New MINI Performance Manual

First published in January 2008

A catalogue record for this book is available from the British Library

ISBN 978 1 84425 122 3

Library of Congress catalog card no. 2006921759

Published by Haynes Publishing, Sparkford, Yeovil, Somerset, BA22 7JJ, UK

Tel: 01963 442030 Fax: 01963 440001
Int. tel: +44 1963 442030 Int. fax: +44 1963 440001
E-mail: sales@haynes.co.uk
Website: www.haynes.co.uk

Haynes North America, Inc.,
861 Lawrence Drive, Newbury Park,
California 91320, USA

Jurisdictions which have strict emission control laws may consider any modifications to a vehicle to be an infringement of those laws. You are advised to check with the appropriate body or authority whether your proposed modification complies fully with the law. The author and publishers accept no liability in this regard.

While every effort is taken to ensure the accuracy of the information given in this book, no liability can be accepted by the author or publishers for any loss, damage or injury caused by errors in, or omissions from the information given.

Printed and bound in England by J. H. Haynes & Co. Ltd, Sparkford

New MINI Performance Manual

Tim Mundy

contents new MINI performance manual

MINI is simply the perfect car for tuning. This has been so from the very earliest Minis through to the very latest versions of the MINI. My father, John Cooper, was the creator of the original Mini Cooper and Cooper S, and my role has been to continue the family tradition with the Cooper models of the BMW MINI.

My first involvement with tuning Minis came with the relaunch of the Mini Cooper in 1989/90 and the subsequent development of the S and S Works tuning packages, which successfully carried on up until the end of Mini production in 2000.

The launch of the New MINI was an unrivalled event – surely no other car in history ever managed to generate such a phenomenal mixture of nostalgia and brand-new enthusiasm. I was delighted that BMW wanted to continue the Cooper name for the performance versions of the MINI, and that John Cooper Works was chosen to develop and market the Cooper Works and Cooper S Works packages. These packages took over three years to research and develop and I was personally fully involved from the beginning. In

addition to the Works packages JCW has designed and produced a full range of tuning parts and accessories to compliment the Works Conversions, and these are available through MINI dealers. Many of the conversions and accessories are fully detailed in the pages of this book.

In 2002, in memory of my father and to celebrate his many years of involvement with both the old Mini and the beginning of the new MINI, I created the John Cooper Challenge, the first ever motor racing series for the new MINI. It is a low-cost formula intended for both novice and experienced drivers and it has proved to be very popular. The next season will include the latest versions of the MINI as well as models made from 2001–2006.

Minis old and MINIs new are quite unique in the automotive industry. The design can only be described as brilliant. I am extremely proud that John Cooper Works remain the only official tuners of the New MINI, and long may our association continue.

Mike Cooper, *December 2007*

Many people helped me with the writing this book, and I am very grateful for their assistance. I would like to thank especially, in no particular order:

Natalie Wakefield and Elyssia Graymore at MINI
Mike Cooper
Richard de Jong and all the staff who worked at John Cooper Works
Nathan King and staff at MINI dealers North Oxford Garage
Monty Watkins and Karen Drury at *MiniWorld* Magazine
James Sutton and everyone at Mini Speed
Steve and Lee Whitton at MED
Trevor Langfield at Wizards of Nos
Adam Block at AmD
Tony Franks at MINI Motorsport Centre
Everyone at the original Mini Mania UK branch in Newport
Everyone at Castagna Milano coachbuilders in Italy
Steve Rendle, at Haynes Publishing

Introduction

Swift but subtle – the MINI Cooper S Works.

Soon after its launch by BMC almost 50 years ago the Mini proved itself a worthy candidate for modification and, spurred on by the works team's early successes in competition, there grew an aftermarket tuning and accessories industry which continued to flourish throughout the Mini's long life, and is still going strong. It turned out that a cult car had been born; and in 2001 it was reincarnated as the new MINI (an independent brand within the BMW Group), a car for which (by contrast) tuning packages were being developed by John Cooper Works long before it was launched. BMW use capital letters for MINI, and throughout the book this style will be retained to distinguish it from references to the old Mini.

The aim is to cover the tuning methods and equipment currently available at the time of writing. Additional upgrade equipment is being researched, developed and introduced all the time by many independent manufacturers, both in the UK and overseas. (The MINI is available in over 70 markets worldwide, ranging from China to Mexico.) As John Cooper Works are the only official BMW MINI tuning suppliers, their works conversions are featured fully, and also included is the wide range of upgrade parts available from BMW, plus the mechanical and electronic upgrade equipment and body parts and accessories available from the large number of tuners and specialists who cater for the MINI.

The background to MINI tuning

No book on tuning the MINI would be complete without a brief insight into the origins of what has become something of an automotive art form. (A more detailed account can be found in the opening chapter of *You and Your New MINI*, also published by Haynes.) The story dates back to 1959 with the launch of the Morris Mini Minor and the Austin Seven, two cars which were identical but for their radiator grilles and badging. Not long before, the fuel shortage resulting from the Suez crisis of 1957 had led to the appearance of 'bubble cars' – small, economical, low-cost cars fitted with what were basically motorcycle engines. This prompted BMC to brief their designer, Alec Issigonis, to design a car to 'knock all the bubble cars off the road'. (It's interesting that one of the most popular bubble cars was the Isetta built by BMW, so BMW unwittingly played their part in the birth of the original Mini.) It hadn't been Issigonis' intention to design a sporting saloon, but with its independent suspension and front-wheel drive the Mini's handling was so good it just cried out for more performance than the standard 850cc engine could provide. And it soon received it.

The most significant part of the original Mini story, as far as the new MINI and its tuning potential is concerned, was the introduction of the Mini Cooper in 1961. John Cooper was the man behind this, and the legend continues today with the MINI under the direction of his son Mike. The more powerful Cooper S arrived in 1963 with a 1071cc engine, 970cc-engined versions were also available for a short time before the capacity was increased to 1275cc. The Mini was extremely successful in virtually all forms of motorsport. The Abingdon-based BMC Works rally team, with the Mini Cooper and S, achieved more than 55 (58 if the unfairly disqualified Monte Carlo win of 1966 is included) class and outright wins in international rallying, and this success earned the team a place in *The Guinness Book of Records* as the most successful rally team of all time.

BMC Special Tuning produced conversion kits, and the Stage One kits could be fitted without affecting the new car warranty. All types of tuning gear were available from BMC

When BMW bought Rover, the Classic Mini was available from the factory with numerous options.

Special Tuning (which became British Leyland Special Tuning) well into the 1970s, and from many aftermarket suppliers as well – many of those names will be found in this book as they have also become involved with the new MINI. There was a huge Mini 'revival' in 1989 spearheaded by the 30th birthday celebrations. The best news of all concerned the relaunch of the Cooper following a successful Cooper Conversion which was available for 998cc cars. Kits soon became available for the 1275cc Cooper, first in the form of an S conversion, and later S Works. The S Works conversion developed by John Cooper Works is available today for the new MINI and, like its predecessor, it can be fitted without affecting the new car warranty.

The Mini must be able to claim the title of the most modified car of all time and, despite having ceased production seven years ago, at the time of writing its popularity is if anything gaining in both numbers of modified cars being built and in the degree of modification being attained, resulting in new examples emerging from both commercial and home workshops around the world, certainly weekly if not daily.

The Classic Mini must be the most modified car of all time. This is the author's 1430cc Mini.

As this degree of popularity is found with very few cars of the thousands of makes and models that have come and gone over the last century, any successor to the original Issigonis Mini design had a great deal to live up to. The Mini was different and managed to remain so for 41 years of production, during which time the basic shape and appearance of the car changed very little. To continue that tradition the new MINI also had to be very different from all other cars – this isn't something easily achieved in current times. Fantastic handling was, of course, a prerequisite.

BMW bought Rover in 1994. There were a number of reasons for this, but the most important (certainly as far as this book is concerned) was that they wanted the Mini. It was a strange twist in the history of both companies, as back in the 1920s, under licence from the Austin Motor Company, BMW produced the Dixi, a version of the then Austin Seven, the original ancestor of the Mini. This tradition was maintained with the launch of the specially-equipped MINI One Se7en in June 2005. Under BMW's ownership in the 1990s, the original Mini was extensively re-engineered and marketed much more as a fashion item with a huge range of factory-fitted and dealer options and accessories. There had always been a massive aftermarket accessory business and now the manufacturer was getting in on the act. This was and is very typical of BMW, and in the case of the Mini it played a big part in setting the scene for the new model and the way in which it would be marketed.

The MINI was launched in Britain in July 2001. Europe had to wait until September that year, and the United States, Australia and Japan had to wait until spring 2002. The first to appear on the scene in Britain were the MINI Cooper and the MINI One. Unlike its predecessor the MINI was an immediate sales success, and by the end of 2001 over 11,600 cars had been registered, almost 20 per cent more than BMW had anticipated. By August 2004, 500,000 MINIs had been produced.

Like its predecessor, the MINI set new standards for driver involvement. It's this which makes it the ideal car to tune for both road and competition. Build quality is very impressive too; it's fully up to the standards expected from BMW but in a smaller package. This is one of the advantages of a car built by a prestige manufacturer. BMW quality shows through, and the bodywork fit and finish is outstanding – the panel gaps are even and the paint quality is probably higher than any other car in its market sector and most sectors above. The

The MINI continues the trend.

MINI is also the first front-wheel-drive car ever to be made by BMW who, although they have made four-wheel-drive cars, are very much committed to rear-wheel-drive. This is probably the main reason why the MINI is marketed as a separate brand. Although the original Mini design fundamentals have been carried forward, technically the MINI is very modern and uses numerous electronic systems. BMW point out, though, that the Issigonis concept of a wheel at each corner, a low centre of gravity, wide track and relatively long wheelbase – all vital ingredients of the driving dynamics – are still present. This is particularly remarkable considering the size of the MINI. It's only 10cm shorter than the BMC 11/1300, it's longer than the Metro and wider and taller than both.

To sum up, the MINI has managed to be different from anything else on the road; it's a bold and very individual design. In this way, coupled with excellent handling and loads of grin factor, it's very much a chip off the old block.

MINIs can easily be transformed. Here is a standard MINI One.

radical body mods and a turbocharged and supercharged Cooper S, there's something for everyone. All mods to MINIs, genuine or aftermarket, or a mixture of both (large and small), will be enormous fun.

The first thing to do is decide upon the style of modified MINI you would like: the Aero kit look; rough and ready; a rally or race replica; or a full Zeemax style body kit, perhaps with a luxury interior. The ultimate must be a coachbuilt MINI from Castagna Milano in Italy. You may prefer to buy an already modified car or a Cooper S Works and further improve upon it, or buy a standard car and start from scratch. The other thing to consider is whether to build a concours MINI or an everyday user – or maybe even one of each. Be warned, MINI tuning can become dangerously addictive.

Deciding what you want to do

The possibilities when modifying a MINI are almost endless, and whether you intend to go for straightforward tuning, in the form of a Stage 1 remap, together (perhaps) with a set of alloy wheels, or for a full ground up build with

The same MINI One after a few mods have been made.

There's a great deal of fun and enjoyment to be had with all the MINI models, and many owners are happy with their car's performance in standard form – the off-the-peg Cooper S is certainly no slouch. But, as an enthusiastic driver you will eventually want that bit more, and for you there's massive potential to improve and modify your MINI, whichever model you choose – and that potential is growing all the time. Beware, though: extensively modified cars, when sold on, rarely achieve prices that recoup the cost of the modifications made.

Ultimately, your choice will be governed by your budget and what you want to achieve, but buying a brand new MINI is preferable if you're thinking long term. It's important to remember, though, that deviating from approved performance upgrades will certainly affect, and could well invalidate, the manufacturer's warranty – this will be dealt with in greater detail later on.

the MINI range

There are, at the time of writing, five versions of MINI to choose from, if the Convertible (with its three different engine options) is considered as one model. Whichever one you buy, you cannot fail to enjoy it. Not one of them is bad; it's simply that some are faster and some more economical than others.

Even in unmodified form (unlike the majority of modern cars) you will want to drive your MINI for the sheer pleasure it gives, rather than just having it to get you from A to B, and whatever the model the MINI has street cred in spades.

Apart from your budget, your age can be a decisive factor in the choice-making process. If you're a young driver, you'll know that getting insurance on any car is difficult, and probably close to impossible in the case of a Cooper S. Although some insurance companies are more tolerant than others, modified cars are harder to insure than standard models. This is particularly the case with upgraded engine performance, and young drivers may find it better to start with modifications to bodywork, suspension, brakes and wheels, and leave engine tuning until later.

If you're looking for more than the test drive your local MINI dealer can offer you, then as an enthusiast living in the UK you can put the Cooper and S through their paces at the BMW Performance Centre at Rockingham in Northamptonshire. Participants must have held a full UK driving licence for at least one year. The experience consists of a briefing on racing lines and techniques, followed by 17 minutes driving on the track with an expert instructor teaching how to push the car to its limits. (All safety equipment, including a crash helmet, is provided.) Afterwards there's a debriefing session. This is well worth doing to find out the capabilities of the Cooper S in standard form. Younger enthusiasts can also have a first driving experience in a MINI One in safe, controlled conditions away from public roads with an ADI instructor. Participants are taught the basics of driving and how to perform manoeuvres such as reverse parking and an emergency stop in groups of three students per vehicle. There's no age restriction, although the guideline is 12 to 16, but the minimum height is 4ft 10in.

MINI One
The MINI One is the entry level Mini and, according to most of the specialist tuners, it's the most popular model to be tuned in the UK (after this comes the Cooper S and the Cooper). With cars in general, base models

often don't get looked after very well, with the consequence that after just a few years the mechanicals and bodywork begin to show signs of neglect. So far this doesn't seem to be the case with MINI One, as most are cared for and cherished just as much as all the other models in the range.

Perhaps one of the main appeals of the MINI One is that at first sight it doesn't really look very different from the Cooper. In standard form the MINI One is in monochrome, which looks good and, in theory, with the exception of its sister car the MINI One D, distinguishes it from the other models in the range. However, some purchasers of Coopers and Ss order their cars in monochrome.

Other more definite distinguishing features of the standard MINI One are the black radiator grille centre and the black vinyl finish door mirrors. But, whilst the standard-fit wheels are 5.5x15in steel with silver-finished plastic hubcaps and 175/65R15 tyres, in the UK and many other countries the majority of MINI Ones are ordered with optional alloy wheels.

Many owners further dress up their MINI Ones either to individualise them or to make them more closely resemble the MINI Cooper. This is very easily achieved and is ideal for younger drivers, or indeed anyone who seeks to create the look and prestige of owning a

Cooper without the problems of an increased insurance premium.

Inside, the One has the same layout as all new MINIs. The seats are trimmed with Aqua cloth fabric, and the steering wheel adjusts for both rake and height (the driver's seat is height adjustable). There's no lumbar support adjustment unless the optional leather upholstery is specified. The rear seats split 50/50.

Standard equipment includes a service interval indicator, a tyre pressure indicator and, as with all MINIs, four airbags, four disc brakes, Electronic Brake force Distribution, and Cornering Brake Control.

The 1598cc engine in the MINI One is exactly the same engine as fitted to the Cooper, but the power output is reduced by the engine electronics to 90bhp, something which is easily rectified! With 103lb ft at 3,000rpm it pulls well and is a very flexible engine.

The suspension set-up of the One and Cooper models differs in that the One has a softer front anti-roll bar, and that an anti-roll bar isn't fitted to the rear. The One also rides 8mm higher than the Cooper models, and the suspension is noticeably softer than the Sports Suspension of the Cooper – even so, the handling is still very good and it's immense fun to drive. On the road, when compared to models further up the MINI range, the softer

The MINI One. This is a very early pre-launch press car.

suspension does result in some increased body roll through fast bends and corners but this isn't a problem, especially when taking the lower power output of the engine into account. Take the MINI One onto a race track and the roll is a lot more noticeable, and tyre grip will be lost correspondingly sooner.

Some drivers prefer the One to the Cooper. It's every bit as enjoyable to drive as all of the rest of the range, even though it may not be as fast. Speed isn't everything in a MINI, and in a lower powered car it's easier to use the full potential.

Summary
- Same great overall MINI looks
- Cheapest to buy
- Five-speed manual transmission or six-speed automatic
- 0–62 in 10.9 seconds with manual transmission; top speed 112mph as standard
- Can easily and cheaply be brought up to Cooper performance plus

MINI One D
Although this is a book about modified MINIs and, at first glance, the One D may not seem to be particularly attractive in modification terms, it certainly shouldn't be dismissed. It is tuned by some who want diesel economy, or who just prefer a diesel engine. It is, after all, still a MINI. It is still entertaining, and some

people actually prefer the turbodiesel power delivery to that of the normally-aspirated Cooper. The MINI One D is the first MINI to be factory-fitted with a diesel engine. Its economy and low running costs make it good for high mileage drivers. It's visually very similar to the petrol-engined MINI One, apart from MINI Cooper S sills, larger air intakes for the intercooler in the front panel, a 'D' badge at the rear and the exhaust tailpipe hidden by the rear valance. Inside, the trim and dashboard is the same as MINI One, but the One D is fitted with a rev counter as standard – pre July 2004 petrol Ones were not.

The MINI One D weighs in at only 35kg more than the Mini One, and therefore there are no modifications to the suspension or brakes. The only difference in this department is that, because of the high torque being produced at low revs, ASC+T is fitted as standard to prevent wheelspin on slippery surfaces. MINI One D is fitted with the same 15in steel wheels and 175 section tyres as its petrol-engined counterpart.

That the car is powered by a diesel engine is evident when it's first fired up, but above idle speeds it's almost impossible to tell from inside the cabin of the car whether it's diesel or petrol. The engine is very torquey, which makes the car very driveable and every bit as much fun as the One or Cooper. The One D is

The MINI One D is similar in appearance to the One but is distinguished from the side by the Cooper S sills.

a great car with great performance and excellent fuel consumption, and some owners spec them up from new with Sports Suspension and alloys, and end up with a car which in the end is close to a diesel Cooper. Enginewise, the diesel can be improved, but to a lesser extent than is possible with all of the petrol-engined models.

Summary

- Cheapest to run with very economical 75bhp diesel (58.8mpg combined)
- Six-speed manual transmission
- 0–62 in 13.8 seconds; top speed 103mph
- Some engine performance tuning potential
- In all other respects tunable as the other models

MINI Cooper

The MINI range would never have been complete without factory-produced performance models. The MINI Cooper is very much a 'proper' Cooper, not just a product under licence or a badge-engineered version of the standard car with a couple of go faster stripes. John Cooper, the man who created the original Mini Cooper, and his son Mike were involved from the very beginning with the design and development.

The MINI Cooper is the bestselling Mini in the range, and is the ideal all round compromise between the entry model Mini One and the Cooper S. The MINI commands a considerable amount of interest and respect in its own right, and adding the name Cooper to the equation adds a notable additional amount of street credibility. The performance of the standard Cooper is good, with 25bhp more than the One, but it's probably better classified as a 'warm' hatch rather than a 'hot' hatch.

The Cooper is 1.4sec quicker from 0-60 than the One, and has a top speed 10mph faster. There are also a number of benefits on the equipment side, including alloy wheels as standard. From the front the easiest way to distinguish the MINI Cooper from the other models is the chromium-plated front radiator grille, and below it the stainless steel mesh lower grille.

A white or black roof comes as standard, but some purchasers specify their cars in monochrome. The interior is trimmed in Kaleido cloth, a rev counter is fitted as standard, and the speedometer remains in the central position. In all other respects the equipment and trim levels are much as the MINI One.

Sports Suspension is fitted to the Cooper as standard. As a result the car sits 8mm lower than the One and One D, and this is sufficient to make quite a bit of difference to the handling, particularly in reducing the amount of body roll. The anti-roll bar at the front end is

The MINI Cooper is subtly different from the One with chromed grille and, as a rule, a white or black roof.

stiffer than the bar fitted to the One and One D, and there's also a rear anti-roll bar; these two items further contributing to the lower level of roll in corners. The improvement is even more noticeable on the track, where the Cooper is considerably quicker through the bends than the One models. The steering is the same as the One, with pin sharp response, and the excellent four wheel disc brakes are shared with the rest of the range.

The extra performance of the Cooper definitely gives it an edge when pulling away, and is particularly noticeable and useful when overtaking. The handling is good, and the benefits of the Sports Suspension are noticeable, particularly with the extra 25bhp on tap.

Summary

- The most popular MINI
- Still economical 115bhp engine giving 43.5mpg combined
- Five-speed manual transmission or six-speed automatic
- 0–62 in 9.2sec; top speed 124mph
- Can be tuned to higher power levels than a standard Cooper S

MINI Cooper S

Reasonable though the capabilities of the Cooper may be, for those in pursuit of serious performance, both in standard form and for ultimate potential, it's necessary to buy a

Cooper S. Expectations were high when the Cooper S was launched in the UK in June 2002, and it certainly didn't disappoint. Press reaction was amazing, and the performance and handling received nothing but praise.

The S is the top of the range MINI, and a number of distinguishing features make it stand out as such. The most noticeable of these is the bonnet scoop, which isn't just a styling feature – it also forms part of the air intake scoop which directs cool air under the bonnet and over the intercooler. As a result, the S bonnet sits 40mm higher than that of the standard MINI and Cooper.

The S bumpers are colour coded as are the rest of the MINI range, but are of a modified design to assist engine cooling and air flow, and there's a black honeycomb grille in the front bumper through which air is channelled into the engine compartment. The rear of the car sports two chromium-plated exhaust tailpipes in the middle of the bumper below a black honeycomb grille.

Along the side of the car the sills are of a more aerodynamic design, and there are two 'S'-badged chromium-plated side grilles with white side indicator repeaters. Other S distinguishing features are a retro-styled chromium-plated fuel tank filler cap and a roof spoiler in roof colour designed to increase the downforce on the rear of the car and improve stability at high speeds. 6.5x16 X Lite

The Cooper S, the ultimate standard MINI.

alloy wheels with 195/55R16V tyres are fitted as standard.

Inside there are two-tone cloth sports seats, the driver's being height adjustable. Many Cooper Ss are fitted with optional leather upholstery, which includes lumbar support on the front seats. Other goodies fitted to the S as standard include a leather steering wheel, a stainless steel foot rest to the left of the clutch pedal and a leather and chrome gearknob. Because the S is likely to be an attractive proposition for thieves, there's an electronic immobiliser and Thatcham-approved Category 1 alarm.

The biggest difference in the S is in the performance. The early Ss produce 163bhp at 6,000rpm, resulting in a 0–60 time of 7.4sec, while later cars produce 170bhp. The S engine produces over 100bhp per litre, an achievement it shares with the E46 BMW M3. Torque peaks at 155lb ft at 4,000rpm, with 80% of the maximum torque being available between 2,000 and 6,500 rpm.

Power delivery is exceptionally smooth and progressive, and as a bonus the supercharger produces a very pleasant sounding whine; from inside the car the sound is not dissimilar to that heard inside an international rally car round a special stage.

The drive is transmitted via a six-speed Getrag manual gearbox, as the Rover-derived box fitted to the One and Cooper wasn't capable of handling the torque from the supercharged engine.

The suspension is Sports Suspension Plus, an uprated version of the Sports Suspension package which is standard on the Mini Cooper. The Plus means stiffer springs with reinforced anti-roll bars on both front and rear axles to further improve handling and reduce body roll during hard cornering.

The S is fitted with ASC+T to prevent wheelspin – something that can be easily achieved without trying in the S.

Summary
- The most receptive to modification
- Sharper handling as standard
- Many used Ss are already high spec
- Six-speed manual transmission
- 0–62 in 7.4sec; top speed 135mph

MINI Cooper S Works
Many Cooper S models are fitted with the BMW-approved S Works conversion developed by John Cooper Works. The conversion became available from April 2003 and basically turned what was already a fast MINI into a seriously fast MINI. The S Works conversion can be fitted to any MINI Cooper S by any franchised MINI dealer. From 2005 the S Works conversion became available as a factory-fit option on new Cooper S models. Full details of the conversion and how it's carried out are given in the Works Tuning chapters.

Approved performance – the Cooper S Works.

Summary
- Even more exclusive than the standard S
- Even more fun to own and drive
- Retains value better than some aftermarket tuned MINIs

Special Edition Cooper S GP

Rumours about a very special lightweight high-performance MINI, the MINI equivalent of the BMW CSL models, had been circulating from quite soon after the original launch of the MINI in 2001. The rumours turned into reality in July 2006 with the launch of the MINI Cooper S with John Cooper Works GP Kit.

The MINI Cooper S with John Cooper Works GP Kit is a two-seater MINI produced in an exclusive colour combination; Grey-Blue metallic combined with a Pure Silver roof and Chili Red wing mirrors. The air scoops on the bonnet and in the front apron are also finished in Pure Silver. Only 2,000 GPs were being built in total for the worldwide market, with approximately 20 per cent of them staying in the UK.

Modifications to the intercooler, as well as engine tuning measures, have increased the power output of the supercharged 1.6-litre engine on a standard MINI Cooper S Works by 8bhp, giving a power output of around 218bhp. This equates to 136bhp per litre. The maximum torque of 245Nm is transmitted to the road by a limited-slip differential. Dynamic Stability Control is fitted to the GP as standard.

The performance of the GP is further boosted by a 40kg weight reduction. This reduction in weight from the standard MINI Cooper S is achieved by modifications to the chassis, the most significant being the longitudinal control arms on the rear axle being made of aluminium. Removal of some of the sound-deadening material and the deletion of the rear seats make a further contribution to the weight reduction.

A number of additional safety and interior options are fitted as standard to the GP. High-performance John Cooper Works red-lacquered brake calipers on the front wheels boost the stopping power. The GP features specially-designed lightweight 18in alloy wheels. Standard upgraded interior equipment includes Recaro sports seats, a single CD player, air-conditioning and a multi-function steering wheel.

Summary
- The most exclusive limited-edition production MINI
- Good long-term classic potential and value retention
- Modified as standard

The Cooper S Works GP (*BMW Press*).

First to go topless – an early Cooper Convertible.

MINI Convertible model range

The MINI Convertible is available with three engine options to correspond with the petrol-engined model line up; 90bhp, 115bhp and 170bhp S. It was introduced in June 2004, the S version later in August 2004. It's one of the ultimate summer fun cars, in Cooper S form maybe the ultimate. It's a four-seater, the same as the fixed roof models. There's no diesel option in the Convertible, and although other diesel convertibles are beginning to appear, it's probably unlikely to happen in a car as small as the MINI. The One Convertible's top speed is 109mph and 0–62 takes 11.8sec; the Cooper achieves 120mph and 0–62 in 9.8sec.

The central locking operates on the doors and boot lid in the usual MINI fashion, but on the Convertible also operates the fuel flap, the windows, the sliding roof and the roof as a whole. The boot lid hinges downwards on these models in the style of the original Mini.

The doors use the same frameless windows.

The standard upholstery in all three versions is cloth, with leather options on all. The dashboard finish is available in silver and anthracite, with further options of wood and aluminium. A rev counter is standard across the range.

The Convertible roof covering is coloured black on the MINI One, but is available in a choice of three colours – black, blue, and green – on the Cooper models.

With the roof in the closed position, the MINI Convertible sits slightly lower than the fixed roof MINIs. The roof can be set to any position within the range of its opening before continuing on to form part of the complete folding roof. Both are electrically operated at the touch of a button and the entire roof will open and stow fully in 15 seconds.

The sliding roof can be opened up at speeds of up to 75mph to the maximum open position of 15¾in or 40cm. There are no catches to be released prior to pressing the operating button, making operation of the sliding roof safe when the vehicle is travelling.

The roof folds to the rear, the pillars retract automatically into the body of the car, as do the rear side windows, all at the same time. The mechanism folds the roof in a Z formation into three layers and stows itself behind the rear seats.

There's also no need for a tonneau cover as the roof is designed in such a way that the front section creates a cover and protects the roof lining. Park Distance Control is fitted as

Cooper S Convertible looks good with the roof up …

standard throughout the Convertible range. There's also a roll bar made of high strength aluminium built into and around each of the rear head restraints. This serves as a roadster-type styling feature which fits in well with the MINI design, as well as being a safety feature.

Chrome line finishing is available as an option on the Convertible, the main difference being that on the Convertible the chromium plating is extended to include the rear seat roll bars.

The MINI One Convertible is fitted with 15in steel wheels in line with the other One models, although most will have the alloy wheel option. The MINI Cooper Convertible is fitted with 15in seven-hole alloy rims of as standard. Both models are fitted with 175/65 R15 tyres. The Cooper S Convertible comes with the 16in X lite alloy wheels from the fixed roof S as standard.

Summary
- Every bit as tuneable as the saloon models
- Great summer fun and open air motoring
- Choice of engines
- Unbeatable style

MINI Automatic
Both the MINI One and MINI Cooper are available with automatic transmission. Automatic models can be tuned in exactly the same way as manual models, with very good results.

… or down.

The Convertible boot hinges downwards in traditional Mini style.

MINI options packages

Three different options packages were offered on the MINI. The packages were known as Salt, Pepper, and Chili.

- The Salt Pack, available on the MINI One and One D only, included front foglights, a height-adjustable passenger seat, the interior light package, Brilliant Silver interior trim, on-board computer, a rev counter (this was standard on the One D and it's reflected in the price of the pack), storage compartment package and velour floor mats.

- The Pepper Pack was available on the MINI One, One D and MINI Cooper. It included all of the items listed above in the Salt pack, plus 15in 8-spoke alloy wheels and chrome line exterior. Inside, there was also perforated leather steering wheel and gearknob.

- The Chili pack was available on the MINI Cooper and Cooper S, and included all the items in the Pepper pack plus, for the

Cooper: 16in 5-Star alloy wheels, cloth/leather Kaleido upholstery, a 3-spoke sports leather steering wheel, a leather gearknob, a rear roof spoiler in body colour, sports front seats, and Sports Suspension.

And, for the Cooper S there was all this, plus an upgrade to 17in S-spoke light-alloy wheels, cloth/leather Satellite seat coverings, manual air conditioning, and Xenon headlights with headlight washers.

There are many different options …

… of interior design for both upholstery and dashboard across the range.

2004 improvements

BMW M3 design on the MINI in the form of the door mirrors.

When the MINI Convertible was introduced in July 2004 there were a number of revisions to the rest of the MINI range, billed as a refresh for MINI One, MINI One D, MINI Cooper and MINI Cooper S. These revisions included redesigned front and rear bumpers, which were fitted to the One and Cooper models. The Cooper S models retained the original sports-style bumpers. At the front, the bumper was lowered, while at the rear the rubbing strip was split, with the fog light repositioned neatly between the two halves – previously the rubbing strip was a single unit with the fog light above.

Reversing lights were integrated into the newly-designed rear light clusters. Redesigned headlights also feature on the Convertible and, from its introduction, also go across the range. All MINI models received new clear glass headlights that provide brighter illumination. The optional xenon headlights were also modified to include an additional ring of light spots for increased visibility.

There were a number of interior improvements. Those most relevant to a modified MINI included an additional side-mounted sun visor for the driver, improved side support from the seat bench side bolsters, the addition of a passenger grab handle above the window, and a larger rear view mirror. The clock was repositioned from its place in the headlining to the central instrument panel. ISOFIX and CD preparation came as standard, and a rev counter became standard on the MINI One. Upholstery options were increased to 14 different cloth, cloth/leather and full leather designs.

There were also some technical modifications and performance improvements. All MINI One and MINI Cooper models came with a new five-speed Getrag gearbox with modified gear ratios. The modification resulted in improved acceleration for both models. Torque on the Cooper was up from 149Nm at 4,500rpm to 150Nm at 4,500rpm, knocking 0.1 of a second off the previous 0–62mph time of 9.2sec. Acceleration in fifth gear from 50–75mph is one second faster at 13.5sec. Power output on

the Cooper S was also up by 7bhp, bringing it up to 170bhp at 6,000rpm, and the top speed up by 3mph to 138mph. The 0–62mph time was reduced by 0.2 seconds to 7.2sec.

buying a new MINI

Although this book is primarily about the (for want of a better description) 'original New MINI' – which ceased production in 2006 – it is, of course, possible to buy a new 'Mark 2' version of the car. At the time of writing, upgrade parts were still being developed, but the principles of modification and range of parts and accessories available from MINI dealers remain much the same.

The big advantage of buying new, apart from knowing how your car has been driven and treated from day one, is that you will be able to buy the exact car of your choice, in your colour and with your own personally selected optional extras (the average MINI customer spends 18 per cent of the total price of the car on factory-fitted options – and 2.5 million variations of MINI are on offer!)

Just about all options for the MINI are available across the range – so you can, for instance, specify Sports Seats and Sports Suspension on MINI One to make it look racier. Virtually everything is interchangeable across the petrol-engined range, although there are a number of differences in the Cooper S engine.

The difficult part, of course, is deciding which options to go for without going wildly over budget. There's certainly plenty to consider when buying a new MINI, and plenty more to think about adding afterwards.

buying a used MINI

One thing about buying a used MINI is that you won't have to join a queue (it can be several months wait for a new MINI). Another is that you'll get the extras already on the car (very few if any MINIS are supplied completely standard) for far less than if you were buying new. The options packs, Salt, Pepper and Chili, make some difference but the most important extras to look for are air conditioning, and items such as alloys on the MINI One and MINI One D.

With the exception of the more recently introduced convertibles, there's a ready selection of all MINI models in the used car market. You will find that, backed by BMW's reputation, they hold their value well, and are likely to continue to do so.

Without doubt, the best source of a used MINI is MINI Cherished, the official BMW-backed approved used MINI scheme, available only at franchised MINI dealers.

MINIs offered for sale by independent dealers, or privately, are nearly always slightly cheaper and can prove to be a good deal, but they must be very carefully checked as there will often be a less comprehensive warranty or, in the case of private deals, no warranty at all.

Buying a car which you intend to improve and modify can be done in one of two ways depending upon the style and degree of modification which is to be carried out. One way is to buy an immaculate example and upgrade it accordingly. The other is to buy a MINI which isn't in such good condition, perhaps with a high mileage and requiring work to bring it up to standard.

Needless to say, the second way will be cheaper and is ideal if extensive mods are to be carried out. As the MINI gets older, more models will fall into this category, but at the time of writing the majority have been well cared for. However, very few cars that have covered even an average mileage will be completely mark free. Those that have been used on motorways will have stonechips on the bonnet and front end, and those that have been parked in car parks on a regular basis will more than likely have dents and scratches from inconsiderate door openers in the cars alongside.

If you're intending to repaint the car, then a few dents and scratches won't matter; similarly, scuffs and damage to the bumpers are irrelevant if you plan to fit an Aero kit, or other body kit. Many of the main areas to check when buying a used MINI (covered below) will apply more to MINIs being bought privately than those from a dealer's forecourt.

The engines in all MINIs have so far proved themselves to be very reliable units in all states of tune. The normally-aspirated petrol engines do sound slightly harsh at high revs when they're being pushed, but this is perfectly normal and is nothing to worry about. Some members of the motoring press have complained about it, but one tuner pointed out that it's actually part of the appeal of the engine. The Cooper S engine has a characteristic whine which is quite normal and actually sounds good.

A lot of the potential faults to look out for may seem relatively minor in themselves, but if a number of them are present the cost of rectification, particularly if the work is carried out by a dealer, will soon add up. As a rule, MINIs with numerous faults are best avoided unless they're very cheap, as there are plenty of others in good condition from which to choose.

New latest model MINIs are available from franchised dealers. Franchised dealers also supply BMW-backed approved used MINIs under the 'MINI Cherished' scheme.

Right: Check the front bumper, particularly at the corners, for scuffs and other damage.

Far right: Rear bumpers too often show signs of damage.

Right: The black plastic arch extensions are also vulnerable, but are relatively cheap to replace.

Right: Scratching to the painted area is annoying.

Right: The side skirts take a pounding from stones, particularly when the car is repeatedly driven over loose surfaces.

What to look for: body

■ As a rule, the overall condition of the bodywork will give a good indication of how the car has been treated. A lot of small dents and stonechips can indicate that the car has had a hard life, and if this is the case then the chances are that it may not have been driven particularly carefully either, so components such as the clutch may be excessively worn.

■ Look down the side of the car in good light and check for dents and scratches. Fortunately such damage is easily repaired these days using localised smart repair systems. The majority of MINIs on dealers' forecourts, particularly franchised ones, will have had this sort of damage repaired. Quality dealers generally don't buy in abused cars in the first place as the need for pre-sale rectification reduces their profit margin.

■ Check carefully for signs of badly repaired accident damage. Examine the body panels for

any signs of rippling. Panel fit should be good, with very even door, boot and bonnet gaps.

■ Unlike the original Mini, the new MINI shouldn't be suffering from serious rusting, but if possible take a look underneath the car, since some earlier models are showing signs of surface rusting to the subframe areas. Although this isn't serious it's something to keep an eye on. It's worthwhile applying rust preventing fluid to these areas, even on a new car, as it will prevent any

problems in the future. A coating of a tried and tested cavity wax, such as Dinitrol which has proved in tests to be very good, is the best solution.

■ Ideally, all plastic trim and the chrome work should also be in good condition. However, if it isn't, most of it can be replaced at no great cost. Particular areas to check are the gutter trims – make sure they're clear of dirt build-up; their condition will give an indication of how well the car has been cared for and whether it has been kept clean all its life or just given a quick valet ready to be sold.

■ If a sunroof is fitted, check the fit of the seal, both outside and inside – some have been known to leak, and rectification can be difficult.

■ The top seal of the front windscreen is another problem area. On early MINIs in particular the seal had a habit of parting

company with the car and flapping in the wind when moving along. Easing out the seal and refitting using a little silicon sealer usually cures the problem, and this should also stop any water leaks into the car; so don't reject a MINI on this point, merely negotiate a small reduction in price.

■ Although quite a few MINIs will be found to have had aftermarket wiper blades fitted, the original BMW-supplied parts are best and are much the same price as the aftermarket items. The windscreen itself should be checked for small stress fractures, as should the black trims fitted to the A, B and C posts.

■ At the rear of the car, check that the high level brake light is properly attached as the housing can split and allow moisture in. The rear light clusters can also let in water – any condensation or green areas, particularly near the bottom, are sure signs that this is happening. The side repeater indicators can suffer the same way.

■ It's very important to ensure that the headlight adjustment motors are working. They can seize through lack of use and should be used occasionally, in the same way as an air conditioning system, to prevent problems occurring. The manual adjustment is situated near the steering wheel. Xenon headlamps should adjust themselves when the lights are on while driving along. Check that they do. Headlight adjusters aren't covered by warranty!

Right: Early Minis suffered from the top screen sealing rubber becoming detached.

Below: At the rear of the car, check that the high level brake light is properly attached. The housing can split and allow moisture in.

Far right: Check the rear lights for moisture ingress and green staining.

- Headlight power washers can easily block, as can the rear wash-wipe, and also to a lesser extent (as they're used more regularly) the front windscreen washer jets.

- The wing mirrors can work loose, so hold each of them and check for excess play which can be caused by the spring mechanism failing.

What to look for: interior

- The interior is generally made of good quality materials and shouldn't show signs of wear and tear even in high mileage MINIs, although those that have been badly abused may have rattles and loose trim items, also scuffs and tears to the seat facings.

- Some softening and shining is to be expected in MINIs fitted with leather trim, and this is most often found on the driver's seat. Check the outer edges of the front seats, again especially the driver's side, for scuffing and wear caused by getting in and out of the car. Look at the join between the seat base and squab, the covers can tear where the seat folds.

- Another important point to check is the tilting mechanism on the front seats; the cables can break and rectification requires the fitting of new seat runners.

- Also check that the frameless door windows rise and fall as they should when the door is opened and closed. If they don't, but the window mechanism is working, the system can be reprogrammed by placing the key in the door and holding in the lock position for 20 seconds.

- The door panels mark easily if abused and, while looking at the doors, check the door check straps; these can become weak.

- Check the rear seat folding mechanism and listen out for rattles from there, and the boot area in general, during the test drive: many do rattle.

Leather wears well but can become scuffed and 'baggy' after high mileages.

Half leather seats generally wear well.

Cloth interiors are generally hard wearing too.

A multi-function steering wheel is nice. Check for high mileage 'shine' around the rim.

Most MINIs are fitted with floor mats which protect the carpets. This is a good thing, but they can also hide damaged carpets. The front carpet is stretched slightly when fitted to the floor and can split along the 'transmission tunnel' edge. This split will be completely hidden by the mat, so it's important to lift the mats to check.

Check the carpets for damp. A number of MINIs have had problems with water leaking into the passenger compartment at the front. The water is soaked up by the carpet which remains wet most of the time – not good for the long term survival of either the carpet or the car.

The most common entry point for water is the door seals, so lift them and check for rust underneath. If light rust or staining is present, it suggests that the seals are leaking.

Check that the air bag warning light works as it should.

While sitting in the driver's seat, start the engine and turn the steering from lock to lock; listen for any rattle or knock, the presence of either probably means that both top and bottom halves of the steering column need replacing. The power-steering pump will make some noise, if possible listen to the pump on several MINIs as a comparison and check that the pump isn't making excessive noise.

One further point to check if you aren't planning on upgrading the factory supplied ICE: early MINIs which were fitted with Radio WAVE sometimes pick up interference from the CAN BUS wiring network, and this is audible through the nearside front door speaker. The best way to check for this is to play a CD that you know well and listen for a ticking noise in the music. MINIs which were affected in this way should have been upgraded to Radio BOOST and have the wiring converted accordingly under warranty.

What to look for: mechanicals

Make sure that the bonnet release mechanism is working correctly. It should operate precisely and release the bonnet first time.

The overall appearance of the engine does give a clue as to how well the car has been looked after. It should look reasonably clean and presentable. Check the oil level and check for any signs of overheating and any unusual noises when test driving.

Look at the ABS pump located on the passenger's side behind the airbox. The CAN BUS wiring loom is routed under the pump bracket and can chafe through – a worn casing, or signs of rust on the bracket or the loom, indicates the need for attention. This was only a problem on some early production MINIs. If the wiring chafed

Right: Mats protect the carpets and, if worn, can be replaced for an instant tidy up. Check that the carpet isn't split underneath.

Far right: Listen for an excessively noisy power steering pump.

A tidy engine bay is a sign of a well-looked-after car. Particularly important if buying privately.

through completely it became impossible to turn off the ignition and the engine remained running.

■ There should be no oil leaks or drips of oil on the ground after the test drive. MINIs aren't known for this, but it's normal practice to check.

■ MINI gearboxes are generally good and don't normally show any signs of wear or make unusual noises – if it does, find another car to buy. The early French-sourced (Rover) gearboxes fitted to the MINI One and Cooper are nothing like as strong as the later 2004-onwards Getrag and Cooper S (also Getrag) 'boxes. Whereas the earlier boxes are OK under normal driving conditions, including normal fast road use, they don't last well under repeated hard driving or racing conditions, so it's possible that problems will be present in a very hard-driven road car. All manual gearboxes should feel precise and positive. Some early Mini One and Cooper boxes had problems with

reverse gear selection, this is often caused by the selector cables being out of position. Rectification is a case of removing the heatshield under the car and cable tying the cables back in the correct place. There's no synchro on reverse gear on these gearboxes. If engaging reverse is noisy, either double-declutch or select first before selecting reverse – the latter is the method recommended.

■ Both the suspension and brakes on all models are reliable, with no commonly known faults, but it's important to be sure that everything is working as it should be, with no unusual clonks or noises. Check that the brakes are effective, and that the suspension is firm – it should feel firmer on Coopers and cars with optional Sports Suspension, and Cooper S models. Brake disc and pad wear is common on very hard driven examples, particularly Cooper Ss.

■ Check for power steering leaks, and take a general look at the suspension components

Alloy wheels often suffer from kerb damage.

and bushes. At the rear the brake pipe can pop out of its mounting near the seat belt mounting point. If this has happened it can be cable-tied back into position.

- Take a careful look at the condition of the wheels, particularly alloy wheels, and look for signs of damage from kerbing. Replacement wheels aren't cheap, and damaged rims suggest that the previous owner may have been a poor driver.

- The condition of tyres is important as they aren't the cheapest around. Make sure that they're in good condition with no cuts or scrapes and that they have plenty of tread left. Worn tyres could be a useful bargaining point though.

Summary
The amount of checking described above may seem rather daunting, but it's extremely unlikely that any MINI will be suffering from all of the problems! Many of them may not be relevant if extensive modification is planned, or if wheels and tyres are to be replaced, for instance, but their existence may help a lower price to be negotiated.

Legal stuff
The same rules apply to buying a used MINI as they do to any other car. This is particularly important when buying privately or from a non-franchised dealer. It's vital to check the identity of any MINI. The registration document should have the seller's correct name and address, and it's worth checking past MoT

certificates and the service history to verify the mileage, and that the car is genuine. Telephone the MINI dealer who has serviced the car to verify the mileage and that the service record is indeed genuine – this can only be done if the car has been serviced throughout by a franchised dealer. To avoid buying a car with a hidden history it's worth having it checked. This will help to ensure that it hasn't been recorded as an insurance write off, has been involved in a major accident, is stolen, or that it has outstanding finance on it. This is particularly important with a recent model car like the MINI, as large sums of money are involved, especially with recent highly specced Coopers and Ss. In the UK this means calling the AA or HPI who will, for a fee, check the vehicle for you and offer a guarantee against many of the above-mentioned problems before you buy.

Maintenance and TLC
The timing of service intervals on the MINI is determined by the car's electronic system. The information is displayed on a service level indicator, so there's no excuse for anyone forgetting to have the car serviced. Mileages between services will vary to quite a degree according to the type of use and the driving conditions and driving style of the owner, but generally speaking the first service will be required between 10,000 and 12,500 miles, with subsequent services required every 15,000 to 20,000 miles.

UK customers of new MINIs can opt to purchase MINI TLC. For a one-off charge of £100 (correct at the time of writing) scheduled servicing is covered for up to five years or 50,000 miles. TLC is available to both fleet and private customers and represents outstanding value, and very few, if any, MINIS are bought without it. TLC is transferable to the new owner if the car is sold during the period, so a customer buying a three-year old MINI with TLC will still have two years of free servicing. This is another reason why the prices of used Minis remain strong. Any recent MINIS under three years old without the TLC package should be avoided. The service history of a MINI which has been regularly serviced by a MINI dealer can be checked with any MINI dealer.

Warranties

Tuning the engine, and possibly other areas of a MINI, will almost certainly invalidate the manufacturer's warranty. The only permitted tuning within the MINI warranty is that which is offered by John Cooper Works and available from JC and some MINI dealers. Careful consideration should therefore be given before embarking on any aftermarket tuning if your MINI is still within the warranty period, and the warranty is important to you. This is also something to consider if buying an already tuned MINI. It's worth noting that some independent suppliers offer a warranty of their own which in some cases will cover those parts of the car no longer protected by the manufacturer's warranty. Check the terms and conditions of any warranty offered by an independent supplier. The back-up warranty offered by MiniMania, at the time of writing, is very comprehensive. It's also a good idea to discuss your upgrade plans with your MINI dealer.

Buying tuning equipment and services

MINI enthusiasts are lucky in that there are many companies throughout the world that can tune the MINI, and many more that can supply tuning equipment and accessories. A number of them are very good. Many of the original Mini tuning companies are both developing and selling equipment for the MINI. The big names, such as Mini Spares and Mini Sport, offer a large range of parts and accessories. Mini Speed, Avonbar, and MED (the last of whom are famous for their A Series engines) are also offering MINI performance equipment and packages. MED have just launched a new division of the company which will specialise in new MINIs, plus a number of other current model tuneable cars such as VW.

Another VW specialist who has carried out a great deal of development work on the MINI is AMD. It's both interesting and good to see

reputable companies, and these include BMW specialists such as Hartge and West, tuning and also developing and producing upgrades. Long-established Mini specialists Mini Mania in the US are also into new MINI in a big way, and have just opened up a branch in the UK who will tune the original Mini but are specialising in the new MINI.

When choosing a company, check out their reputation. Generally, those that have been around a long time will have built up a good reputation or otherwise. There's a list of some of the suppliers in the appendix at the back of the book. Check that warranty position, too, if it's important.

Safety

Some of the alterations you make on your MINI will be cosmetic, but many will be mechanical or electronic upgrades aimed at improving performance. It's important to consider the whole car, which means when making your MINI go faster you also need to upgrade its braking and handling. In fact, the brakes and suspension must be upgraded before any serious engine tuning work is undertaken. Most of the modifications and improvements detailed will adversely affect the safety of your car if the work isn't properly carried out by a competent person.

Masses of genuine upgrades and enhancements are available, and some MINI dealers can supply both parts and help with fitting, but for more radical and specialised tuning it will be necessary to enlist the help of an independent specialist. Above all, if you have any doubt as to your ability to carry out any of the work, then you should entrust it to a qualified and reputable MINI dealer or competent MINI specialist.

Insurance

Upgrading the performance of a MINI will affect your insurance. It's essential to obtain a quote from your insurance company before carrying out any work. Some insurance companies are more tolerant of modifications than others, and some may offer discounts to club members.

The Cooper Works was the first MINI upgrade from John Cooper Works.

Except for the One D, the original Mark I MINI power unit is a Chrysler-built four-cylinder petrol engine (the Pentagon) developed by Chrysler and BMW specially for the MINI, and manufactured in Curitiba, Brazil. It's a smooth and responsive unit in all its variations in the range. The One D is powered by a Toyota 1ND-TV unit from the Yaris; A four-cylinder 75bhp, 1364cc, 16-valve turbocharged and intercooled diesel engine with second-generation common rail technology. Like the petrol engine, it was further developed by the BMW Group. All the engines are mounted transversely and drive the front wheels in true Mini tradition.

The petrol engines have a cast-iron block with a 77mm bore and 85.8mm stroke. The 16-valve aluminium head has an overhead camshaft which is driven by a maintenance-free timing chain – BMW prefer timing chains to cam belts. All can run on unleaded petrol between 91 and 98 octane, meaning that special adjustments don't need to be made for different markets around the world.

Engine management is taken care of by a Siemens Powertrain Controller. This controls the throttle by wire technology in place of mechanical cable linkage. When the accelerator is pressed, the information is passed to the Powertrain Controller which increases the fuel supply to the engine. The Controller also monitors engine torque; if the required torque is below the maximum potential, the controller will retard the ignition timing to provide a rapid pick up which will be noted by the driver particularly at lower speeds.

The MINI One and Cooper petrol engines

The One and the Cooper are actually fitted with exactly the same power unit, but the Cooper has the benefit of an additional 25bhp. The extra performance to justify the Cooper name has been obtained by upgrading the electronic engine management system, rather than the fitting of any uprated or tuned mechanical components. From July 2004, modifications to the transmission increase engine flexibility in the mid range, improving torque and acceleration figures.

Tuning potential

Because it starts off with a lower power output, the power increase potential of the One engine is greater than that of the Cooper but, as the engines are the same, the ultimate tuning level is, needless to say, the same. Tuning the One to Cooper performance levels and slightly above is simple and inexpensive, and is achieved by electronic upgrade. Small improvements can be made to the Cooper engine using similar methods. More radical tuning is possible, including the fitting of an uprated cylinder head and camshaft. The ultimate mod is to fit a turbocharger, and this is all dealt with in future chapters.

The Cooper S petrol engine

The fitting of a supercharger and intercooler to the engine in the Cooper S resulted in 163bhp at 6,000rpm, a considerable improvement over the 115bhp output of the normally-aspirated Cooper. In the 163bhp MINI Cooper S the Pentagon engine design remains the same, but the crankshaft, connecting rods, pistons, engine bearings and valves have been uprated to cope with the increased thermal and mechanical loads produced by the supercharger.

An oil cooler, albeit a very small one, is fitted and there's splash oil cooling of the pistons to provide additional engine cooling and lubrication.

Apart from the big improvement in performance figures – the Cooper S manages 0-62 mph in 7.4sec, compared with the Cooper's 9.6sec – the engine produces over 100bhp per litre, an achievement that the Cooper S shares with the E46 BMW M3.

The advantage of using a supercharger as opposed to a turbocharger is that there's no turbo lag to delay throttle response. Forced induction produced in this way provides a significant increase in engine power which in the S is delivered exceptionally smoothly and progressively. Torque peaks at 155lb ft at 4,000rpm, with 80% of the maximum torque being available between 2,000 and 6,500rpm. The intercooler is supplied with air from the air scoop on the S's bonnet.

Supercharged power units can be prone to engine knock, but this is overcome on the S's engine by reducing the compression ratio to 8.3:1 (from 10.6:1). Another system, Active Knock Control, also monitors the combustion process, allowing the engine to run smoothly on unleaded fuel with an octane rating of anything between 91 and 98. A different uprated exhaust system is also used with twin exhaust tail pipes.

The Cooper S successfully complied with all UK emissions legislation. The engine was one of the few in the market not requiring secondary air injection or exhaust gas recirculation in order to comply. Transmission is through a specially designed 6-speed Getrag manual gearbox, as the Rover-derived 'box fitted to the One and Cooper wasn't capable of handling the torque from the S's supercharged engine.

Tuning potential

There's much that can be done to upgrade the performance of the Cooper S. Small mods to the supercharger and a remap will provide reasonable gains and beyond this there's plenty of potential to add around 100bhp of additional power to the original engine output whilst still retaining driveability and reliability. Power gains beyond this cause additional problems not least actually putting the power down on the road through the driven front wheels.

The MINI One D diesel engine

The One diesel engine develops 75bhp at 4,000rpm, and the maximum torque of 133lb ft is developed at just 2,000rpm. The engine is able to build up two thirds of its maximum torque at 1,500rpm, which means that the fun element – which is a lot of what the Mini is about – is still very much present.

The high torque at low revs is typical of a modern diesel engine and makes the MINI One D ideal for both city driving and for long runs. The fuel economy is excellent with a combined cycle figure of 58.9mpg. This means that, depending on driving style, the MINI One D is able to travel in excess of 600 miles on a full tank of fuel. The official urban consumption figure is 48.7mpg, and in extra urban conditions 65.7mpg. These figures mean that the MINI One D is the most fuel-efficient production car to be built by the BMW group. (Tuning car engines can be about improved economy as well as improved performance, and often both.) Even with good fuel consumption there's no performance penalty – top speed is 103mph, 0–62mph acceleration in 13.8sec, and accelerating from 50–75mph in fourth gear takes 12.3sec, all very reasonable figures for a small 1.4 diesel-engined car. Like all MINIs, when being driven it feels quicker than the figures suggest.

The engine has a bore of 73mm and stroke of 81.5mm. The engine block and cylinder head are made of aluminium which helps keep the weight of the MINI One D down to 1,175kg compared with 1,140kg for the petrol-engined MINI One. The MINI One D engine uses lightweight pistons that run in liners made of grey cast iron. There are four valves per cylinder and an overhead camshaft. The compression ratio is 18.5:1.

The camshaft is driven by the crankshaft via a maintenance-free timing chain, like the MINI petrol engines. Two independent poly-V-belts drive the ancillaries, such as the alternator, water pump and air-conditioning compressor; also the servo pump on the hydraulic power steering – the electro-hydraulic steering fitted to the petrol-engined cars isn't fitted to the One D. There's a damper at the front end of the crankshaft which absorbs the diesel engine vibrations to help minimise the transmission of vibrations to the drive belts.

The second generation common rail diesel technology is one of the modifications to the Toyota engine made by BMW. It incorporates intelligent computer-controlled Bosch fuel injection to supply fuel at exactly the right time and under extremely high pressure directly into the combustion chambers. Like the petrol cars, Mini One D has a wire-free throttle.

The turbocharger compressor runs at speeds of up to 225,000rpm and compresses the fresh air to an overpressure of 1.2 bar. To overcome the resulting heat problem, the air is cooled by an intercooler before it reaches the combustion chamber. An intercooler is fitted next to the engine radiator and receives its supply of air through the radiator grille. The One D is fitted with a quick start pre-heater system, and there's also an oil/water heat exchanger that maintains correct temperatures and helps prevent the engine oil from ageing prematurely.

From September 2005 the MINI One D engine power output was increased by 20 per cent. This translates into an additional 13bhp, which knocked nearly two seconds off the 0–62mph time. The power unit was thoroughly revised and offers the same economy as its predecessor. The combined fuel consumption figure remained the same at 58.9mpg. The power increase came from a revised engine management system and fuel injectors, as well as exhaust gas recirculation with a large capacity catalytic converter. Torque has been increased by 10Nm to 190Nm and is now available between the engine speeds of 1,800 and 3,000rpm. The top speed is 109mph, and the engine complies with EU4 emission standards.

Tuning potential

The tuning potential of the One Diesel is more limited than that of the petrol engines. A worthwhile gain can be obtained from remapping the ECU, and exhaust system mods, which also produce an increase, are possible. The tuning potential beyond this hasn't been developed as most people wanting serious power will opt for the petrol-engined MINIs.

tuning the engine – an overview

As soon as new MINIs became available, the independent tuning sector began researching how to extract higher levels of performance from the engines. Tuning kits for the new MINI are now readily available from many of the traditional BMW tuning companies, and also from the majority of the traditional Mini tuners. A considerable amount of development work has gone into performance upgrades for all MINI models, but understandably the bulk of the work has been geared to the Cooper S where the greatest performance gains are to be had.

Many owners have opted to go for the John Cooper Works conversions because, apart from the historical links and well-developed performance packages, the upgrades retain the official MINI three-year warranty. With new and nearly new MINIs this will continue to be the case, but as MINIs start to age and become more readily available at attractive prices it's likely that the alternative market will expand considerably. In fact, all the signs are that the new MINI tuning market may ultimately end up larger than that of the original Mini.

Much of the early work centred around electronic upgrades as this is by far the fastest and most economical way to obtain higher power, but we're now seeing a number of traditional tuners working together to develop certain areas of the engine. At the time of writing extreme developments on the cylinder head and fuelling side were being explored. Some tuners have attempted to extract more power by boring out the engine, and 1800cc conversions have been tried by more than one tuner, but not so far with a great deal of success.

Engine removal

MINI engines can on the whole be modified in situ, but should removal be necessary it isn't actually difficult as the front end of the car comes away quite easily (see the section on building a Works Cooper S) allowing excellent access to virtually everything.

MINI engine compartment with engine unit removed.

works tuning

John Cooper Works

Of all the specialist companies offering tuning, upgrade packages and components for the MINI range, there's only one with the official backing of BMW to produce faster Coopers whilst still retaining the full manufacturer's warranty. That company is John Cooper Works.

The link between Cooper and the original Mini goes back to 1961 with the introduction of factory-produced Mini Coopers and Cooper Ss. This lasted for ten years and came to an end in 1971, but, much to the fans' delight, the Cooper was reborn in 1990 when a bolt-on tuning package was developed and sold by the then John Cooper Garages, eventually renamed John Cooper Works (JCW) and run by the late John Cooper's son Mike.

It's not surprising, with the Cooper name legendary in motorsport, that BMW not only chose to continue to use it for the faster models in the new MINI range, but also involved John Cooper and his team from the early stages of its development.

JCW's involvement was strictly with the Cooper Works side of MINI, and they didn't produce Works or tuning packages for the MINI One.

The Cooper Works conversion kits are supplied by JCW and could be fitted either by them or by a franchised BMW MINI dealer. Many owners used to make the pilgrimage to the JCW garage in East Preston, Sussex, to have their conversion fitted, as it made their car seem just that bit more special.

However, in 2006 Mike Cooper decided to close the JCW garage at East Preston and concentrate on the design and development of tuning kits. At the time of writing, all JCW tuning packages are still available from MINI dealers. Also, Tony Franks, who had been JCW's chief engineer, has set up his own specialist MINI preparation business in Shoreham by Sea, and carries out race preparation on the John Cooper Challenge cars.

MINI Cooper Works

The first of the new Works MINIs was launched by JCW in November 2001, just four months after the MINI Cooper itself was launched by BMW. It had been developed at the same time as the MINI itself, and it had taken the development team at Cooper nearly three years to perfect. *Autocar* magazine enthused over it, announcing that 'The real MINI Cooper is back'.

Cooper Works cars have proved very popular, with 1 in 9 Cooper Ss being converted to Works specification.

In the late 1990s BMW had enlisted the help of John and Mike Cooper and the team to not only help develop the production cars but the higher performance conversions too. The Cooper Works conversion retains the full BMW MINI warranty, and it's a very good reason to choose this conversion, rather than one of the aftermarket kits, if you're buying a new or a nearly new MINI which still has plenty of manufacturer's warranty left. Additional peace of mind also comes from the fact that the conversions were comprehensively tested before they were launched in much the same way that new cars are put through their paces. This involves operating in extremes of temperature, plus many miles being covered under differing conditions to ensure reliability. In the case of the Works MINIs this added up to 150,000 miles of durability testing and 20,000 miles of high-speed testing at racing circuits such as Spa, Goodwood and the BMW Williams test track. This type of testing is necessary for the factory warranty to remain in place. Reliability and longevity of the vehicle are as important in this conversion as the performance enhancement.

The Cooper Works – officially called at launch The John Cooper Works MINI Cooper – is a step between the Cooper and Cooper S. At the time, the Cooper S wasn't available and the Works Cooper was the fastest BMW-backed MINI available. The Works conversion package consists of a mixture of traditional tuning components and electronic tuning. There's nothing radical involved, and it's really just some fine tuning of the engine to extract smooth usable extra power. It would probably equate to a Stage One tuning kit in old fashioned tuning language, and this is also true when compared with stage tuning today. At 127bhp it's close to the Stage One packages offered by the independent tuners.

At the heart of the conversion is a modified cylinder head; this consists of a reworked brand new casting and new components; not an exchange item. The head is modified in the traditional way by grinding away metal to reshape the inlet and exhaust ports to improve the flow characteristics. JCW say that the inlet ports have been reshaped to allow the gases to

flow in as straight a line as possible into the cylinders. The amount to be removed, as with any cylinder head modification, is critical – remove too little and there's barely any advantage, remove too much and power will be lost.

With the Cooper head, more work has to go into the exhaust side than the inlet, and in total around 20 hours is spent modifying each head. This work includes matching the inlet ports to the manifolds. The heads are CNC machined, and computer aided design was used extensively in their development. As well as the improvements to gas flow, the compression ratio is raised slightly from 10.6:1 of the standard Cooper to 10.9:1. The cylinder head mods contribute in the region of a 12bhp increase in power, and the rest of the power is obtained by the fitting of a less restrictive air filter assembly and a freer-flowing stainless steel exhaust system from the catalytic converter backwards. The tailpipe is fitted with a chrome-plated finisher and looks considerably more aggressive than the standard fitment. The system not only helps to improve power, it also changes the note of the engine, making it sound very much more purposeful. The standard exhaust manifold remains as it is. To change it would involve the catalytic converter and could affect emissions.

The engine is also remapped, and a CD is supplied with the conversion for this purpose. The remapping is necessary to bring the management side of the engine in line with the modifications that have been made, but also changes are made to the way that the engine responds – these changes give improved throttle response and more mid-range torque. The car is still very smooth, but is much more willing to rev, and there's more power higher up the range.

Adding the Cooper Works package to the MINI Cooper makes quite a difference, and that difference is a lot more noticeable when the car is driven than it is on paper. Looking at the performance figures you might be excused for thinking there's not much difference between a standard Cooper and a Works, but this isn't the case in reality. Right from the beginning, when the engine is fired up, there's the exhaust note. It's quite a bit racier and just a bit noisier, thanks to the modified freer-flowing system, and this immediately makes the car feel more powerful; but there's a great deal more to the car than that. BMW's official 0–62 time is 8.9sec.

The MINI One and Cooper have received some mild criticism in that the engine tends to become slightly coarse when it's pushed hard. The improved torque band of the Works Cooper helps to overcome this. There's still plenty of the low range torque that is a feature of the standard car, but the Works Cooper has more torque higher up the rev range. This probably results from the gas flow improvements to the cylinder head. The uprated engine is generally much more willing to rev, and throttle response is improved making for an altogether racier engine – the revs fall away faster too. There are no suspension modifications to the Cooper Works; being a Cooper the MINI sports suspension is fitted, making the car lower and stiffer anyway. The suspension handles the extra power easily, and shows off the capabilities of the standard system, although there's no reason why the handling of the car shouldn't be further improved using the suspension packages now available from Cooper (detailed later on).

As a finishing touch to the package, subtle but nonetheless important JCW badges are added to the car on the two dummy grilles on each front wing, and on the bootlid. There are also two works badges, one included on the identifying plate located under the bonnet.

Many Cooper Works cars are supplied with a BMW bodykit and numerous other additional accessories. A large range is available from Cooper.

The MINI Cooper Works conversion takes one full day to fit. It's still readily available through JCW and it's also fitted to the John Cooper Challenge race series cars. Fitting of the Cooper Works package to roadgoing MINIs has slowed down somewhat since June 2002 for the very good reason that this was when the 163bhp Cooper S was launched. The price difference between the S and the Cooper Works was minimal and the standard S was far quicker.

MINI Cooper Works v standard Cooper performance figures

Model	0–62mph	50–75mph 4th gear	top speed
Cooper	9.2sec	10.5sec	125mph
JCW Cooper	8.9sec	10.1sec	126mph

MINI Cooper S Works
The MINI Cooper S is respectably fast in standard form. It's undoubtedly the ultimate fun car in its class and has been hailed as such on many occasions by the motoring press. But for owners who seek even more power and enjoyment from their MINI, yet retaining the full BMW factory warranty, there's the Cooper S Works. The S Works conversion became available in April 2003, and since then has proved to be a great success, with more than one in nine Cooper Ss being converted to Works spec in the UK market. JCW had at the time of writing converted over 11,000 Ss at their premises alone.

From 2005 it became possible to order a brand new Cooper S Works from a MINI dealer, the conversion being carried out at the build stage in the MINI production plant at Oxford. JCW converted both new and used Cooper Ss, the ratio of new to used being around 50/50. The work required to turn a standard Cooper S into a John Cooper Works S takes ten hours and is completed in one and a half days.

The S Works conversion was developed in much the same way as the Cooper Works

The S Works pack is fitted to John Cooper Challenge race cars. This car is undergoing conversion at the Cooper Works in East Preston, Sussex.

package, and it took a similar length of time to perfect. Again, before the product was launched, extensive testing was carried out, including subjection to extreme temperatures ranging from 35°C right down to −20°C, which really should cover the temperature bands likely to be encountered by the majority of people wanting to drive a performance MINI.

The Cooper S Works is modelled along the same lines as the Cooper version. There are no drastic modifications to the engine, no massive overbores or uprated camshafts, and all the uprated parts are bolt-on. This is to ensure that the S package can be fitted by any franchised MINI dealer.

Like the Cooper Works, at the heart of the Cooper S Works is the modified cylinder head. The modifications are along broadly similar lines to the Cooper Works head: work is done to the inlet and exhaust ports, and the chambers are slightly reworked and polished. Compared to a standard head the difference is immediately noticeable. The modified head is a brand new component rather than being supplied on an exchange basis – and the Works conversion is usually carried out on brand new or virtually new cars. Valve sizes in the modified head are

the same as the standard car, and the camshaft is also the standard item.

What makes the big difference to the extra performance of the S Works, though, is the modified supercharger, the main modification being a different driving wheel, but internal mods are also carried out as the supercharger spins faster on the Works S. The result is that supercharger boost is up from 0.7bar to 1.0bar. A new drive belt is also supplied in the conversion.

The exhaust system is replaced from the cat back, with the standard exhaust manifold retained for emissions reasons. The replacement exhaust is noticeably faster looking than the standard item. It has an additional silencer to meet noise regulations, but it's very much a straight-through. The system is a parallel flow, low back pressure system; it's tuned not only for improved engine performance but also for improved aural pleasure both inside and outside the car. It doesn't make the car noisy, it just sounds nice, and the S Works passes all noise and emissions regulations easily.

Fire the car up and the upgrade is immediately apparent, the deeper throatier exhaust note revealing that this is a breathed on MINI. This exhaust note stays with you all the way through the range and makes the car feel faster than it actually is; even more so than with standard MINIs.

The engine is remapped to adjust the management system to the modified components and to get the best out of the changed specification. With the very early Works Ss, upon pulling away there was a very slight hesitation (a small hiccup at low revs fairly early on). This was present in the test car used in preparing this book and was a characteristic of all early S Works conversions. JCW say that the engine remapping has since been slightly revised, and that this has eliminated the problem on later conversions, and the S Works is now smooth throughout the range. Even with the hiccup, which isn't a problem once you become accustomed to it, the car was very smooth, especially for a 1600cc engine producing this kind of power. The power and response from the tuned engine isn't so noticeable lower down the range, but it gets on song particularly in the mid range.

In August 2004 the power output of the S Works conversion was increased by 13bhp to 210bhp (154KW) at 6,950rpm. Maximum Torque is 245Nm at 4,500rpm. The uprated conversion was launched at the Paris Motor Show along with a new range of performance parts and accessories from JCW. A number of these upgrade parts were fitted to the factory-produced limited-edition Cooper S Works GP.

The new 210bhp kit boosted the performance of the S Works to provide a 0–62mph of 6.6sec and a top speed of 143mph. The figures themselves appear only slightly better than the previous figures (see the comparison table below) but on the road the difference is very noticeable. Throttle response is a lot crisper and the engine note through the performance exhaust system sounds even better. The good news with the new kit was that the price remained the same, and the labour time for fitting wasn't increased either.

The performance upgrade has principally been achieved through changes to the air filter system, allowing greater airflow at high revs (above 4,500rpm) by triggering an extra air intake flap to reduce pressure losses within the intake system. New fuel injectors and engine management calibration are also fitted to ensure optimum performance and durability under all operating conditions.

The arrival of the new Works kit was precipitated by the modifications made to the MINI Cooper S earlier in 2004, including changes to the gear ratios on the six-speed Getrag gearbox. The new kit is available worldwide, for both the MINI Cooper S and MINI Cooper S Convertible.

Existing 197bhp Works MINI Cooper Ss can have an upgrade fitted (new air filter intake system, injectors and calibration) at any official MINI dealer, for the cost of the upgrade plus one hour's labour for fitting. Both the new kit and upgrade are fully approved by MINI, which means that vehicle warranty and MINI TLC service pack remain unaffected.

The only modifications carried out in the S Works conversion are the changing of engine components. There are no upgrades required to the suspension or brakes. Everything, including springs, dampers, discs and pads remain completely standard. Numerous genuine MINI Cooper upgrade parts are available, however, for those who wish to modify the rest of the vehicle accordingly.

The MINI Cooper S Works can be identified externally by a discreet badge on the mesh grille at the front (located by the number plate), at the sides by badges on the imitation grilles, and at the rear by the badge on the boot lid on the opposite side to the Cooper S badge. In the engine compartment there's a larger intercooler cover, which is again Works badged, and an identification plate fixed behind this to the left of the cooling system reservoir. At the rear the twin chromed Works-inscribed exhaust pipes also give the game away.

MINI Cooper S Works v standard S performance figures

Model	0–62mph	50–75mph 4th gear	top speed
Cooper S	7.4sec	6.7sec	135mph
S Works 197bhp	6.7sec	5.6sec	140mph
S Works 210bhp	6.6sec	5.4sec	143mph

the making of a MINI Cooper S Works

There are many steps involved in the process of converting a standard MINI Cooper S to S Works specification. The sequence below details the main steps and shows a Works kit being fitted to a brand new Cooper S. The car had been delivered to its owner the previous day and driven directly to John Cooper Works to be converted. The changing of the components over to the upgraded items is carried out in the following manner:

Top left: A new Cooper S is driven into the JCW workshop.

Top right: First of all the front end of the car is removed to allow easy access to the engine components. The entire front bumper and lower grille assembly can be removed in well under half an hour.

Above: The next task is to remove the aluminium crossmember which is bolted on in front of the radiator and the air conditioning condenser (where fitted).

Left: The front chassis legs are removed.

Right: The air con condenser can be carefully moved to one side and supported to avoid disturbing the system. The condenser is linked to the rest of the system by flexible hoses to enable this to happen. The cooling system is drained and the radiator removed.

Top right: The oil cooler being moved out of the way.

Right: The front end stripping completed ready for the engine work to begin.

Far right: The drive belts are removed.

Right: The intercooler being removed from the top of the engine.

Far right: The inlet manifold is removed from the cylinder head. This allows access to the supercharger.

Far left: The supercharger assembly is removed, complete with the air intake.

Left: Removing the jump start terminal and the airbox.

Far left top: Removing the offside engine mounting.

Far left bottom: The timing mark lined up ready for removal of the timing chain.

Left: The cylinder head bolts can then be undone ready for removal of the head.

Right: The new modified supercharger complete with reduced diameter pulley.

Far right: The original elbow air intake is removed from the original supercharger and transferred over to the new supercharger.

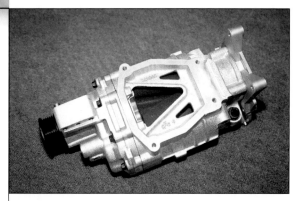

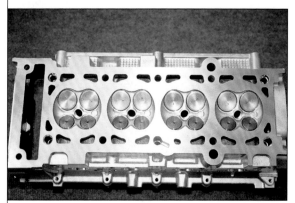

Above: The new modified Works cylinder head.

Right: The chambers are lightly modified and polished which looks good, but most of the grinding and reshaping work is carried out on the inlet and exhaust ports and is therefore internal.

Below: The studs are transferred from the original head.

Below right: A new standard head gasket is used

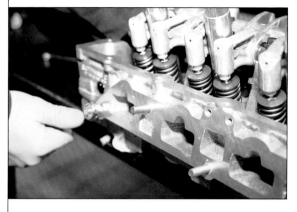

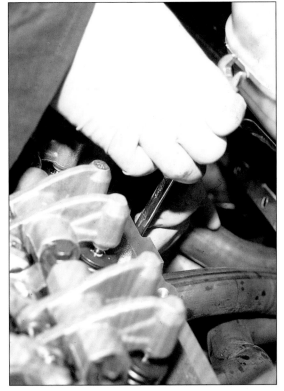

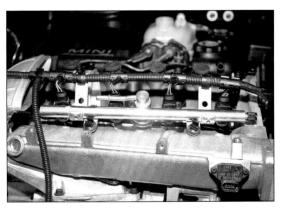

Top left: The new gasket on the cleaned block face. The supercharger and elbow are in situ in this picture.

Top right: The new head being fitted. The head bolts are tightened and the timing chain and pulley fitted in the correct position on the end of the camshaft.

Middle left: Tightening the exhaust manifold to the head. A new gasket is fitted.

Middle right: The new inlet manifold gasket in position.

Bottom left: The inlet manifold and injection componentry refitted to the head.

Bottom right: A new set of spark plugs is fitted.

Left: The intercooler and the JCW casing are fitted. The S works identifying plaque is fitted to the engine, and a final check is made for tightness on all nuts and bolts. The radiator is refitted, the air con condenser and front aluminium crossmember also, followed by the front bumper. The radiator is refilled with coolant and the underbonnet side of the conversion is completed.

Centre top: The later 210bhp kit includes an uprated air intake system and new fuel injectors.

Centre bottom: The standard Cooper S exhaust system is removed from the car at the joint with the catalytic converter and replaced with the new Works system. The new system includes an additional silencer which is closer to the engine end of the system and not shown in this picture. The JCW system is considerably less restrictive than the standard item.

Bottom left: The twin Cooper S Works chromed tailpipes are put on. After this the badges are applied to the bodywork, and S Works identifier strips are fitted on to the door steps to alert all passengers that they are entering an S Works Cooper as they climb on board. The conversion isn't all mechanical: new software is downloaded into the MINI's management system using a laptop. Rolling road tuning isn't necessary, the car is correctly programmed with the downloaded software.

Below: A completed Cooper S Works outside the old John Cooper Works headquarters in East Preston and ready for the road. This car is fitted with numerous Works accessories.

stage tuning

There are also many independent tuners in the market, and for those who decide not to opt for BMW-approved JCW, the most popular way of making a MINI go faster is to fit one of the many stage tuning conversions.

Stage tuning of engines has always been popular, and for the original Mini it dates back to the early days of BMC Special Tuning at Abingdon in Oxfordshire. Back then, many independent tuners offered similar packages, and a large number are still available today. The idea lives on with the new MINI and a number of stages of tune have been developed and are available from many of the independent new MINI specialists.

As a general rule the stages have been designed to allow tuning to be carried out progressively, with each of the stages adding something extra to the previous stage. Tuning the MINI can begin at any stage, or it's equally possible to go straight to the highest stage if the tuning budget and insurance premiums allow. Using a reputable independent tuner is very important when going down this route, particularly if the MINI is still under warranty – check the independent tuner's warranty and try to find out more from people who have had dealings with your intended company before authorising any work.

One of the most comprehensive range of stage tuning packages for all of the models in the MINI range has been developed by Mini Speed, and it's Mini Speed's tuning programme which is detailed here to illustrate the steps available. It's worth noting that Mini Speed will only tune MINIs on their premises to ensure that everything is carried out to their exact specifications. Some companies are prepared to send Stage 1 and 2 conversions to customers by mail order for DIY installation. There's nothing wrong with this; the process isn't complicated and full instructions are included – it's just a matter of individual company policy. A number of tuning components and methods are listed below, e.g. ECU remapping, and processes such as this are described in more detail in the full engine tuning sections in the chapters which follow.

Conversion kits

MINI One
MINI One tuning has proved to be exceptionally popular and currently four stages of tune are available from Mini Speed for this model.

Stage 1 – The MINI One Stage 1 conversion is especially popular because of the amount of gain for relatively little cost. The kit consists of a straightforward ECU remap. The result is a

Stage 1 kit, the device used for reprogramming the ECU.

The box plugs into the OBD (on board diagnostic) port under the steering column.

A prescribed sequence must be followed when remapping.

useful power increase from 90bhp up to 115bhp. This is by far the most popular conversion carried out on the whole MINI range, as it will basically bestow MINI Cooper performance upon the MINI One. Remember, the engine and transmission are identical in the MINI One and the Cooper, and it's only the ECU that creates the difference in power between the two models.

The Stage 1 kit is very easy and quick to install, and can be easily reversed when the time comes to sell the car. The package isn't, however, transferable from one car to another. This is common to all MINI tuning of this nature and it's understandable as it prevents one individual purchasing the upgrade and tuning all the MINIs in his or her MINI club!

Stage 2 – The Stage 2 conversion is again purely an electronic upgrade. It consists of a Phase 2 ECU remap. The result is an increase in power from the standard 90bhp to 130bhp. It's possible to go directly to this stage, or power can be boosted from the 115bhp Stage 1 upgrade.

Stage 3 – The Stage 3 conversion also consists of an ECU remap, but in addition much more extensive and more traditional engine tuning is involved. This is the point at which serious tuning begins, and this will be reflected in the price. A big-valve cylinder head is fitted, together with a fast road cam, an induction kit and an upgraded stainless steel exhaust system. The increase in power is substantial – up from the standard 90bhp to 150bhp.

Stage 4 – The Stage 4 conversion again consists of an ECU remap, a big-valve cylinder head, a fast road cam, an induction kit, an upgraded stainless steel exhaust system, plus a stainless steel tubular exhaust manifold to improve gas flow. This results in a further increase in power up to 165bhp. This is the ultimate road tuning package for the MINI One.

MINI Cooper
Three stage increases are available for the MINI Cooper, following a similar line-up to the packages on offer for the MINI One.

Stage 1 – The Stage 1 conversion for the MINI Cooper is an ECU remap, which provides an increase in power from the standard 115bhp up to 130bhp. This is basically the same conversion as the MINI One Stage 2.

Stage 2 – The Stage 2 conversion is an ECU remap, a big-valve cylinder head, a fast road cam, an induction kit and a stainless steel exhaust system. As with the MINI One Stage 3 conversion, this kit lifts the power output of the Cooper up to 150bhp.

Stage 3 – The Cooper Stage 3 conversion includes the Stage 2 ECU remap, a big-valve cylinder head, a fast road cam, an induction kit, a stainless steel exhaust system, together with the addition of a stainless steel tubular exhaust manifold. Like the MINI One, the power output is boosted to 165bhp. This is the maximum Stage power available for this model.

MINI Cooper S
The MINI Cooper S is the most tuneable of the range, certainly in as much as ultimate power and performance are concerned. Five stages of tune are available from Mini Speed. Because the engine is fitted with a supercharger, slightly different methods of tuning are employed.

Stage 1 – The Cooper S Stage 1 conversion consists of an ECU remap and a smaller supercharger pulley. This pulley increases the supercharger boost pressure by 15psi. Stage 1 provides the Cooper S with an increase in power from the early S output of 163bhp up to 195bhp.

Stage 2 – The Stage 2 conversion is an ECU remap, a smaller supercharger pulley giving a 15psi boost, an induction kit, a raised rev limit and modified supercharger. This kit gives an increase in power up to 215bhp.

Stage 3 – The Stage 3 conversion again includes an ECU remap, a smaller supercharger pulley giving a 15psi boost, an induction kit, raised rev limit and a modified supercharger, plus a Mini Speed upgraded camshaft. This offers an increase in power to 225bhp.

Stage 4 – The Stage 4 conversion includes an ECU remap, a smaller supercharger pulley giving a 15psi boost, an induction kit, a raised rev limit, a modified supercharger, the Mini Speed uprated camshaft, a big-valve cylinder head, a stainless steel exhaust system and a stainless steel tubular exhaust manifold. This provides an increase in power up to 245bhp.

Stage 5 – The Stage 5 conversion is the ultimate conversion on offer from Mini Speed. Like the Stage 4 conversion, it consists of an ECU remap, a smaller supercharger pulley giving an even higher level of boost to 18psi, an induction kit, a raised rev limit, a modified supercharger, the Mini Speed upgraded camshaft, a big-valve cylinder head, a stainless steel exhaust system and a stainless steel tubular exhaust manifold. Additional equipment includes a large top-mounted intercooler with water spray, a modified throttle body and a modified inlet manifold. This kit provides an increase in power up to 260+bhp.

MINI One Diesel
Tuning is also available for the MINI One Diesel. Mini Speed has developed only one upgrade kit.

Stage 1 – Prior to installing the MINI One Diesel Stage 1 kit, a full diagnostic check and rolling road test are carried out. The ECU is then remapped to increase the brake horsepower from the standard 74bhp to between 110 and 115bhp. The effect is to increase the fun factor experienced when driving the One D without increasing the fuel consumption. The conversion provides in the region of a 21% power increase and an 18% torque increase.

Independent tuners
The Mini Speed conversions detailed above illustrate the tuning stage kits available from one MINI specialist. The company you use to supply and fit tuning components to your MINI is a matter of personal choice and recommendation, and you will also be influenced by geographical location.

There follows a selection of tuning packages and car conversions offered by companies throughout the UK, and further afield:

Top Mini tuners MED, in Leicester, launched a big range of MINI stage tuning packages in 2005. They have been tuning original Mini engines for many years and have built some excellent high-performance engines for my own

Minis. As well as engine tuning for the new MINI, they are offering a range of suspension and brake upgrades.

The engine upgrades start with the DV1 kit for the MINI One, which is a remap producing an extra 25bhp and 15lb ft of torque. DV2 adds a high-flow catalytic converter and larger downpipe, which boosts the output by 35bhp and 25lb ft torque. DV3 includes the DV1 and DV2 upgrades plus an MED-profiled Piper cam, a sports exhaust system and a hi-flow air intake. Power is up by an extra 40bhp and 25lb ft of torque. The ultimate MINI One conversion from MED is the DV4, which contains all of the above plus an MED big-valve head, and the result is 45–50 extra bhp and 30lb ft of torque.

A similar range of DV kits is available for the MINI Cooper. Again, four stages of tune are offered. These start with DV1, which adds 10bhp and 10lb ft torque, DV2 adds 15bhp and 15lb ft torque, DV3 20bhp and 25lb ft torque, and DV 4 25bhp and 20lb ft torque. The contents of the kits are basically similar to those fitted in the corresponding stages to the MINI One. Power increases differ slightly because of the already upgraded performance of the Cooper over the One as standard.

It is with the Cooper S that serious stage tuning is possible in the MED line-up, and seven stages of tune are available. DV1 consists of a remap which adds 8–10bhp and 5lb ft torque. DV2 pushes the output up by 35bhp and 20lb ft torque and consists of a remap plus a 15% smaller supercharger pulley and a new Goodyear performance drive belt. DV3 includes DV2 plus a high-flow catalytic converter and downpipe, and a sports exhaust. Power is up by 40bhp and 25lb ft torque. DV4 adds 45bhp and 30lb ft torque, and to achieve this an MED larger throttle body and an air intake kit is fitted, over and above the DV3 components. DV5 produces 55bhp and 45lb ft torque over standard; the extra performance coming from a GRS Motorsport intercooler. DV6 equates to an extra 70bhp and 50lb ft torque; an MED big-valve head is used to achieve this. The ultimate stage of tune from MED is DV7. Power is up by 110bhp and 75lb ft torque. Additional components over the DV6 package are an uprated supercharger and a charge cooler to keep air temperature down, plus a lightweight flywheel which weighs in at 13lb lighter than standard. An uprated clutch is also fitted to cope with the additional power, and a Quaife ATB differential is recommended. The DV7 upgrade is suitable for road or competition. When it's intended for competition use, MED recommend further upgrades to the gearbox and transmission.

Another company that has been tuning original Minis for many years is Mini Sport in

One of Mini Sport's development MINIs.

Padiham, Lancashire. Mini Sport have carried out a lot of development work on the new MINI and offer a number of packages to improve performance, all of which have been extensively researched and developed in-house by their team of engineers and road testers.

Beginning with the MINI One, there's the Phase 1 Tuning kit which is an entry level package designed to increase driveability and performance. The kit includes an engine management upgrade, a K&N sport induction air filter kit and a stainless steel exhaust system. This kit provides a 30bhp gain on the MINI One and a 15bhp increase on the MINI Cooper.

Next up is the Phase 2 Tuning kit which gives an extra 55bhp to the MINI One and an extra 30bhp to the Cooper. This kit again modifies the engine management system and also includes a performance cylinder head, performance camshaft, stainless steel manifold and stainless steel full exhaust system. There's also a sports Catalytic converter and twin silencers.

Mini Sport offer four levels of tune for the MINI Cooper S. The S/E Phase 1 Tuning Kit which is a 200bhp conversion which tunes the supercharger and engine for maximum mid-range punch. This is followed by the S/E Phase 2 Tuning Kit for 220bhp which, in addition to the components in the 200bhp kit, includes a water-to-air chargecooler to ensure air entering the engine is as cold and dense as possible. The new chargecooler sits in place of the original intercooler and is extremely straightforward to fit, with minimum modifications. Moving on up the scale the 235bhp conversion is as the 220bhp kit, with the addition of the uprated Mini Sport S/E camshaft which Mini Sport say provides the S with more usable power and torque, whilst retaining the driveability. There's also an S/E twin-exit exhaust system and an S/E high-flow exhaust manifold which significantly increases the outflow of the exhaust gases from the engine. The S/E twin-exit stainless steel exhaust is unusual, as the sound level is variable according to the owner's wishes. This is made possible by easily accessed removable DD deadeners in the rear silencers.

The S/E Phase 4 Tuning Kit is the ultimate Mini Sport conversion, and produces 250bhp.

Mini Spares were among the first to be involved with the new MINI. This is their development car.

The content is as the 235bhp conversion but with the addition of a big-valve cylinder head. Mini Sport say that they have applied everything that they have learned from nearly 40 years of preparing original competition Minis, together with the latest flow-bench techniques, in developing the head. The combustion chambers are individually shaped and balanced before being polished. The heads come equipped with uprated valves and guides, as well as valve springs and stem seals.

Mini Spares is the world's largest supplier of parts, accessories and tuning equipment for the original Mini. Mini Spares became involved with the new MINI from day one and were among the first to produce a modified MINI Cooper. A number of performance kits are available from Mini Spares, all of which have been developed in conjunction with AmD. There are five stages, Stage 1 (200–210bhp) which concentrates on supercharger mods; Stage 2 (220bhp) adds a Milltek exhaust manifold and system with performance cat; Stage 3 (230bhp) additionally has an induction kit and larger throttle body; Stage 4 (240bhp) adds a gas-flowed cylinder head; and Stage 5 (255bhp) a gas-flowed big-valve cylinder head and lightened flywheel. All of the Mini Spares conversions are set up on the rolling road at AmD's premises at Bicester, near Oxford. AmD also produce upgrades for the MINI One and Cooper and have carried out extensive development work of their own, looking into a number of extreme power options for the Cooper S in particular. Mini Mania are very big in the USA, and have

The new MINI has attracted tuners, new and old. AmD, who have an excellent reputation in the world of VW, Audi and Porsche, have played an important part.

AmD's development MINI.

upgrade started as soon as the S was launched. This conversion, although not BMW-backed like the JCW upgrades, is close to home and most BMW dealers (95%), according to Birds who are the UK Hartge agents, will service the Hartge S under the MINI TLC servicing programme. Having said this, if considering this conversion, do check with your MINI dealer first! The Hartge conversion is a 210bhp upgrade, which is based around modifications to the supercharger and drive assemblies with revised engine management settings, and each modified car is individually mapped.

The new engine management maps for UK customers are programmed and transmitted from Hartge's studios near Merzig in Germany. German customers can have their cars converted and mapped on site. The conversion has TuV approval at 200bhp, although the Birds dyno figures are 210bhp, and figures of 212–215bhp have been achieved in Germany. On the road this translates into a 0–60 time of 6.6sec and a top speed of 144mph.

Hartge conversions are subjected to a number of endurance tests before being released. Hartge also produce an upgrade for the MINI One, which is a software upgrade to increase the performance of the standard engine to just above that of the standard MINI Cooper.

Another conversion that is close to BMW is the upgrade produced by A C Schnitzer. Again this is an upgrade for the Cooper S and is available from some BMW dealers as BMW GB are distributors in the UK of A C Schnitzer products, or it can be obtained direct from A C Schnitzer in Germany. This conversion is also a revised supercharger drive system which drives the supercharger faster at any given engine speed than the standard component. As a result, boost is up and, together with a modified exhaust system, increases power to 193bhp at 7,000rpm, which means a quoted 0–62 time of 7.0sec and a top speed of 145mph.

A well-known UK-based BMW tuner is Ray West. An ex-touring car driver, Ray has produced some interesting supercharged BMWs in the past and has now turned his hand to tuning the Cooper S. The West Tuning S is more powerful than some other conversions,

more recently opened up a branch in Newport, Wales. Mini Mania offer a number of stage tuning possibilities, as well as just about any type of conversion possible on a MINI. Many of their conversions and cars are featured later on.

Many of the stage tuning kits detailed above will appear similar simply because of the nature of this method of tuning. At the risk of seeming repetitive it is, however, interesting to compare the slightly different methods employed by the various tuners as the level of performance increases and the slightly varying results at each level. All of the companies whose products are detailed here are reputable engine tuners and any one of the packages at a particular level should provide impressive results. Specifications and power outputs may vary as packages are further developed.

Some tuners have chosen to launch complete car conversions. One of the first performance upgrades for the Cooper S was produced by Hartge, renowned BMW tuners for many years. Development of the engine

Mini Mania have also produced some impressive development MINIs.

and a greater number of modifications are carried out to the engine. The bottom end of the Pentagon engine is very robust (all tuners agree on this point), so it has been left as standard on the West MINI. The cylinder head has been extensively modified; fully gas-flowed with opened up ports and larger inlet and exhaust valves. An uprated camshaft is also fitted to increase valve lift and duration. On the fuelling side there's a larger throttle body, and the exhaust is replaced with a bigger bore item. Also a new catalyst is fitted which is much freer flowing. Modifications are made to the ECU to provide more fuel all through the range. West Tuning say this combination of modifications produces 243bhp. The improvement is certainly noticeable in the performance figures which are down to under 6sec to 60mph and a top speed in excess of 150mph.

It should be pointed out that when the engine reaches moderate to high stages of engine tune, in order to cope with the extra performance modifications must be made to the suspension and brakes. All of this is covered in later chapters. Most of the higher

tuned MINIS detailed here come with brake and suspension upgrades as part of the whole tuning package. An example is the West tuned car which has upgrades in the form of Leda dampers and springs, which lower the car by 30mm as well as stiffening it slightly. The brakes are upgraded too, with special West Tuning 308mm diameter vented front discs and AP Racing four pot 5000 series calipers.

These are just some of the conversions available worldwide for all models of the MINI. As with all tuning conversions, there are similar lines of thought running in most of them, but there are also a number of interesting differences in both the modified parts and the power output figures. All the companies above are reputable and all figures were obtained on a rolling road. However, they weren't all obtained on the same rolling road and this should be taken into consideration when comparing figures – most rolling roads produce slightly different figures. All figures quoted are those from the tuning companies themselves; the cars weren't tested independently for this book.

The MINI
Siemens ECU.

Both the fuelling and the ignition timing in a MINI are controlled by an engine management system, a small computer or Engine Control Unit usually referred to as an ECU or ECM (Engine Control Module). The engine management unit in the MINI is a Siemens Powertrain Controller EMS2000; this is the MINI's ECU. It monitors and controls ignition timing and the fuelling across a range of driving conditions and also controls the throttle by wire technology, which replaces the mechanical cable linkage.

The smooth increases or decreases in the throttle are managed in a similar way to the operation of a domestic light dimmer switch. When the accelerator is pressed the information is passed to the Powertrain Controller, which then increases the fuel supply to the engine. The Controller also monitors engine torque; if the required torque is below the maximum potential, the controller will retard the ignition timing to provide a rapid pick up which will be noted by the driver, particularly at lower speeds.

The ECU constantly receives a great deal of information about the engine, such as engine speed, fuel mixture, temperature (both ambient and engine), and exhaust gas emissions from a number of sensors around the engine which enables it to vary the ignition timing and fuelling needed to suit the conditions at the time – for instance, when the engine is cold a richer fuel/air mix is required. A number of other systems in the car are also controlled by the ECU, for example the stability control system and the air conditioning. However, for the purposes of performance upgrading it's only the engine management side of things that we're concerned with in this chapter.

Inside the ECU.

electronic tuning

The easiest and quickest way to extract more power from all models in the MINI range is by electronic tuning. It's effectively the same as upgrading the carburetters and ignition system on an older vehicle, but much simpler in that no change of parts or additional setting up is required. All internal combustion engines require the correct ratio of fuel and air to enter the engine and, in the case of a petrol engine, the spark plug to fire at precisely the right moment so that the fuel will be burnt correctly and produce power. The fuel/air mix is injected into the engine on all modern cars via the fuel injection system; in earlier cars this function was performed by the carburettor (or carburettors) and the timing of the spark by the distributor.

The engine management system is upgraded by tuning the ECU, and quite large improvements in performance can be obtained from altering the programming of the MINI's ECU. The process is generally known as remapping (referred to frequently in the earlier sections on stage tuning and the John Cooper Works MINIs). Remapping plays a very important part in the tuning of any ECU-controlled engine, and it's absolutely essential that it's done whenever any engine components are changed or upgraded. It's particularly important with modifications to the supercharger or cylinder head. Failure to remap in these cases can result in incorrect fuelling; in particular the fuel mixture may become lean, which can cause severe engine damage.

Since the performance of a car can so easily be improved in this way, you may well ask why it isn't done by the manufacturer in the first place. The answer is that, with cars produced for a worldwide market, manufacturers have to consider the big picture and design things to suit a perceived average customer for any particular model. So the set-up is going to be a compromise rather than an optimisation of potential, especially as allowance also has to be made for poor quality fuels being used and the possibility of the car being abused during its life through lack of maintenance and proper servicing.

This, of course, leaves scope for individual improvement and, what's more, in the majority of cases power can be improved without any adverse effect upon fuel economy. Also, with careful reprogramming by a reputable specialist tuning company, the long-term reliability of the engine and the rest of the car's components are maintained.

When the ECU is reprogrammed, changes are made to the ignition timing and fuelling throughout the entire rev range; alterations are also made to the fuel mixture and sometimes to rev limits. This type of tuning is used at manufacture by the MINI factory to create differences between models. As has been stated, the MINI One and Cooper engines are absolutely identical mechanically, and the extra power produced by the Cooper engine is obtained purely by different mapping of the ECU, and nothing else.

Producing the new map, as opposed to actually reprogramming an individual ECU, does require expert knowledge and equipment and it isn't something that can be carried out at home. The process can be accomplished reasonably quickly by a specialist if only basic changes are made. However, producing a full remap for a radically modified engine can take days of work, and the results need to be thoroughly tested before the upgraded mapping can be released onto the open market. Highly tuned engines often require an individual map to be designed.

ECU reprogramming isn't just confined to specialist tuning companies; BMW update and improve standard MINI software on a fairly regular basis, and updated software is

A DIY Stage 1 upgrade.

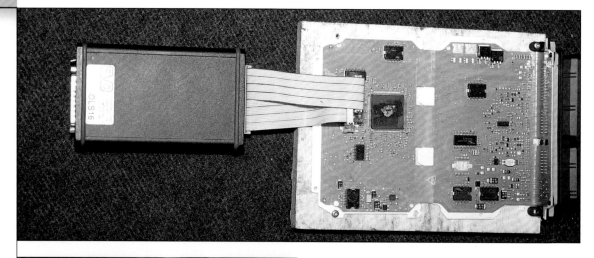

A development
ECU ready for
remapping at
AmD.

Remapping
through the
OBD port.

Main dealer
remote
programming
device.

available by mail order from some tuning companies, as the reprogramming steps are very simple and easily dealt with as long as the instructions supplied with the unit are followed. Many of these units will come from the same manufacturer, regardless of the tuning company from whom you buy the upgrade, but instructions may vary according to the supplier.

Once the system has been reprogrammed, the unit can be reinserted to return the car to its original standard set-up, should this be needed for main dealer servicing or for resale purposes, etc. Changing from higher performance to original, or vice versa, is a quick process and usually only takes around three minutes. This type of electronic tuning is most commonly used in many of the Stage 1 kits to boost the power output of the MINI One to that of the MINI Cooper, i.e. up to 115bhp. Even more popular on the MINI One is the higher increase up to 125bhp.

The result is better acceleration (the car is more responsive with smoother power delivery) and slightly improved top speed; and, depending upon how the car is driven, fuel consumption can improve slightly. Driving style does have a big effect upon this, though. If the extra performance is used to the full all the time, fuel consumption will increase rather than decrease. An important point to note is that this type of software upgrade is locked to the individual car; it cannot be used on any other vehicle, thus preventing one person buying the upgrade and passing it round to others. Straightforward

sometimes loaded during routine servicing at an official MINI dealer.

For DIY remapping there are two methods available. The first and most widely used is the one-click system where a small pre-programmed unit is plugged into the MINI on-board diagnostic (OBD) port, which is located just above the pedals in the passenger compartment. This type of programming is remap conversions of this nature are readily available from a number of specialist companies, including Mini Mania, MED, AmD, Mini Spares, Mini Sport, and Mini Speed, although not all will supply by mail order.

One very straightforward and inexpensive upgrade produced by a well-known company, and available from MED, is Bluefin, which is manufactured by Superchips. Bluefin is a software upgrade that plugs into the MINI's OBD port, and is designed for DIY. Installation is simply a case of following the on-screen prompts; no technical or mechanical ability is required and the performance increase can be removed in exactly the same way. A further advantage of Bluefin is that it can also be used as a diagnostic tool to find faults. Superchips offer a warranty, which covers all areas excluded from the manufacturer's warranty when the upgrade is installed. The system is particularly worthwhile for the MINI One and Cooper, both of which will be boosted by 33bhp.

The other way of remapping is to physically change the chip within the ECU. ECU reprogramming experts AmD, of Bicester in Oxfordshire, say that this isn't an option on a MINI as the MINI ECU shouldn't be dismantled because it's made of soft material internally that breaks easily.

The above describes early stage programming of the ECU. Much more involved professional remapping for really serious engine tuning involves connecting the ECU to a laptop. AmD connect an emulator to the ECU, which allows real-time mods, and takes out any guesswork that would otherwise have to be employed. AmD have an entire department dedicated to this. Once it has been fully developed, the new software can be downloaded into the ECU. All of the more individual ECU upgrades of this nature require testing on a rolling road to ensure that the set-up is absolutely correct before the car is driven on the road.

Remapping the MINI One D diesel engine
Remapping the ECU will also produce a worthwhile gain in the MINI One D, and will make the engine quite a bit more lively. The ECU is remapped using the same methods as with the petrol engines to increase the brake horsepower from the standard 74bhp up to between 110 and 115bhp. This conversion provides in the region of a 21% power increase and an 18% torque increase. This is a very worthwhile gain and creates a car with the same sort of power output in brake horsepower terms as a standard MINI Cooper and is equally as much fun to drive. This is the basis of the Stage 1 conversion offered by a number of MINI tuning companies and described in the previous chapter.

As with similar petrol engine ECU mods, depending upon how the car is driven, there can be a small improvement in fuel consumption, which may be of particular interest to owners of diesel MINIs who mostly opted for the diesel engine for economy reasons.

Ignition system modifications
In any petrol engine the ignition system plays a very important part in extracting maximum performance from the engine. The intensity of the spark at the spark plug will affect the efficiency of the engine from both a performance and a fuel economy point of view. It will also affect the general feel of how the car drives and may also have an effect upon the longevity of the engine. Upgrading the ignition system can produce small but nonetheless worthwhile gains, and there are three areas in which the ignition system of the MINI can be upgraded.

Spark plugs
The first modification to make to the ignition system on all MINIs is to upgrade the spark plugs. There's nothing actually wrong with the standard spark plugs; those fitted to all petrol MINIs are perfectly suitable for standard and mild stages of tune, but above this an upgrade becomes desirable. One upgraded plug which, in both the UK and the USA, has proved to be very successful at improving spark quality is the NGK Iridium IX spark plug. This is a slightly cooler running plug than the standard, and the main difference between it and the standard plug is the 0.6mm iridium centre electrode. The

Upgraded spark plugs produce a small improvement.

iridium electrode provides superior performance and is also very resistant to erosion, which means that the plug in normal use will usually last quite a bit longer than the standard item. Iridium is six times harder and eight times stronger than the standard plug's platinum and also has a melting point 1,200° higher. This means that the electrode can be made smaller, the voltage required is considerably lower, and the ignition will be improved, with less demand placed on the components. Fitting the NGK Iridium plugs should provide a small, but nonetheless worthwhile, improvement in both acceleration and fuel consumption.

Spark plug leads

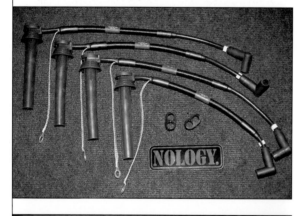

Spark plug leads are the next upgrade after performance spark plugs.

Fitting top quality performance spark plugs is the first step towards obtaining the ultimate performance from the ignition system. The second is to fit upgraded spark plug leads. There are a number of upgraded leads suitable for the MINI on the market. Good quality ones come from companies such as Magnecor, and they're also available from tuning companies: Mini Speed sell their own 9.2mm performance leads. However, the ultimate leads are produced in America by Nology. At around twice the price they aren't cheap, but each lead incorporates a capacitor and separate earth connection. This enables the lead to store energy until it reaches a high level of intensity which is then released in a shorter than normal burst. This provides a very fast and clean burn of the fuel and air mixture in the cylinder. Nology claim that their plug leads provide an increase in spark intensity of over 300%. Nology leads are available in the UK and the USA from Mini Mania.

Ultimate performance 'Nology' spark plug leads from Mini Mania.

Plasma booster

The ultimate ignition upgrade – a plasma booster.

The third way to improve the spark efficiency of the ignition system is to fit a plasma booster. This is a small box which is wired into the ignition system to provide a more powerful spark. It works by increasing the power of the spark and delivering a hotter spark to the cylinder – the manufacturers say up to 100% improvement. It's a simple device to fit and can deliver an additional 4bhp, plus up to a 10% improvement in fuel economy.

the fuel system

The main objective in tuning an engine is to make it possible for the fuel/air mixture to enter the combustion chambers, burn at the right time and for the resulting exhaust gases to exit all in a more efficient way than they would do in a standard engine. The faster the process can be achieved by the engine, the better its performance will be, and the fuel system plays an important part in this. We've already looked at the electronic tuning possible on the MINI engine, which involves the management of the fuelling, and the purpose of this chapter is to look at the physical changes you can make to the fuel system to complement and enhance the electronic modification. This, however, works both ways in that when any significant modifications to the fuel system are carried out, it's both usual and necessary to match the modification with electronic tuning by reprogramming the ECU. Some air filter upgrade mods won't require any reprogramming, but it's advisable to check with the supplying tuner, and also to follow the instructions supplied with any tuning component.

As already said, MINI engine management is taken care of by a Siemens Powertrain Controller EMS2000. This unit plays a key role in fuelling in that it controls the throttle by wire technology which replaces the mechanical cable linkage, and the amount of fuel supplied to the engine throughout the rev range (the system is described more fully in the preceding chapter on engine electronics). All the petrol engines fitted to MINIs must be run on unleaded petrol with an octane rating between 91 and 98. The wide range capability is to ensure that the car can be used without adjustment in different markets around the world where the quality of fuel can vary considerably. The fuel system on all MINIs has proved to be both reliable and efficient in standard form but there are a number of modifications that can be made to the system to improve performance, in addition to the electronic modifications already covered. Although the information contained in this chapter applies to all MINIs, including the diesel where specified, there are many more fuelling modifications which are exclusive to the MINI

Cooper S, involving the supercharger. These are dealt with in detail in the following chapter.

Uprating the air filter

The standard air filter system in a MINI channels air through the grille and into the air filter box. The filtered air is then passed into the engine. The air filter serves two purposes, first to remove dust and other harmful debris before the air enters the engine (failure to do this will result in rapid wear of the engine internals), and second to reduce the noise of the air being sucked in. Without a filter there's quite a lot of noise in the passenger compartment, and when an upgraded free-flow filter is fitted it will result in increased internal noise levels. Fitting an upgraded filter is the first modification that's usually made to the fuel system, and it's certainly the easiest modification. There are many air filter kits available for the MINI from most of the upgraded air filter manufacturers, but a great deal of care should be taken when deciding which filter to fit. Some kits are better than others; some will give a 1–2bhp increase, some can do even better than this, but others will provide no increase in performance and, at worst, some have even been proved to actually reduce the overall power output from the engine. So, take advice and buy carefully, preferably from a supplier who can provide comparison figures obtained on a rolling road. Another consideration is whether a suspension strut brace is either fitted or to be fitted to the car in the future. Strut braces prevent large filter assemblies from being fitted.

Air filter upgrades are available as straightforward replacement elements, and also

Air filter upgrade kit.

Air filter
upgrade in the
engine
compartment.

as more sophisticated induction kits, from most
new Mini specialists and are made by a number
of manufacturers, including ITG, K&N,
Pipercross and Green Cotton.

The simplest form of air filter upgrade is the
replacement element. These are designed to
increase airflow while still filtering the air as
efficiently as the standard item. These types of
filter are often known as 'drop in' panel filters.
Fitting is simply a case of replacing the standard
element with the upgraded item, and is
achieved within minutes.

All of the systems feature reusable filter
elements, which are washable; sometimes this is
with water and detergent, sometimes with a
special solvent, which must be purchased from
the filter supplier as most are particular to the
make of filter. After cleaning, the filters are re-
oiled using specially formulated oil – again, the
filter manufacturer's oil must be used. Apart
from a performance increase, another advantage
of a performance air filter is that, from a running
costs point of view, the reusability of the filter
element offsets the higher cost of the filter
upgrade, as a replacement filter won't be
needed at service time.

More sophisticated air filter upgrades come
in the form of induction kits. The idea of these
isn't only to improve the efficiency and flow
characteristics of the air filter element itself, but

also the speed and volume of air reaching the
filter. These systems take a little longer to install
and the cost is somewhat higher than the drop
in panel variety, but greater performance gains
are to be had, particularly at the higher end of
the rev range. With most of these systems the
original airbox is removed and replaced with
the new one supplied.

Cold air entering the engine is far better for
performance, and some air intake systems,
such as the Mini Mania Ultrik Cooper S system
from the USA, use stainless steel in the airbox
construction, the idea being to reflect as much
heat as possible back into the engine
compartment and away from the air filter, to
keep the air filter element as cool as possible.
The Ultrik S air filter box is also of a wider
design to enable better airflow across the
whole of the filter. The system uses the
standard MINI air inlet from the front grille, and
the vents at the base of the windscreen. The
filter unit itself is a reusable K&N unit. The
Ultrik airbox has a removable plate, which
allows the use of the Ultrik upper front
suspension strut brace.

Alternatives include the Ram-Air Induction
system which is manufactured by Gruppe M
who supply Formula 1 teams. This system is
available from Birds. Intended for fast road and
track day applications, it's designed to produce

accelerated airflow into the engine, and Birds say it will produce an extra 12bhp between 5,800 and 6,800rpm. Numerous other systems are available and many are very good. The choice comes down to individual preference, coupled with evidence of performance gains.

Larger fuel injectors

At higher levels of tune, the fuelling system benefits from larger fuel injectors. These are available from specialist outlets and are a direct replacement for the existing injectors. The Cooper Works S 210bhp conversion uses larger injectors – this level of power increase gives an indication as to the point at which larger injectors are beneficial.

Throttle body modification

In line with the majority of current fuel-injected petrol engines, the MINI is equipped with a throttle body. This is the closest part of a fuel-injection system to a carburettor, and it controls the amount of air and fuel mixture which enters the engine. This flow is regulated by a butterfly valve, which is located within the body. The larger the diameter of the throttle body the greater the amount of air can enter the engine at full throttle. The standard throttle body fitted to all petrol MINIs is 58mm in diameter. Increasing this by fitting a throttle body with a larger internal diameter will provide better throttle response and improved power output, the greatest benefit being felt at the top end, although driveability is generally improved throughout the rev range. There are a number of larger throttle bodies available from specialist tuners. A 62mm diameter Ultrik

throttle body is available from Mini Mania. This increases airflow by 15.7% at full throttle, which is a significant improvement.

Alternatives to the Ultrik body include the modified 63mm throttle body for the Cooper S, which is available from Mini Speed. Mini Speed, like most other suppliers (including the Ultrik body), supply this body on an exchange basis, a surcharge being payable upon ordering and refunded when the original throttle body is sent to the supplier.

MINI One D fuelling upgrades

The diesel engine fitted to the MINI One D is manufactured by Toyota (it's the one the Toyota Yaris uses). Compared to the Yaris, the MINI engine is already modified in standard form. BMW have upgraded the injection system to second-generation common rail with Bosch fuel injection. The first generation original Toyota system was only 1,350bar, and the increase boosts the peak torque figure by 7lb ft. The high pressure assists atomisation of the fuel into extremely fine particles, resulting in quieter, cleaner and more efficient combustion.

Few further mods are available for this engine other than remapping of the ECU and the fitting of a free-flow air filter system. Both remapping and a filter change do produce a worthwhile gain and will make the engine quite a bit more lively. Depending upon how it's driven there can be a small improvement in fuel consumption. Both remapping and air filter upgrades are available from a number of tuners, but not all of them – some tuners prefer to stick to modifying and improving the petrol engines.

Far left: Larger throttle body.

Left: The MINI One D fuel-injection system.

forced induction

There are two different ways of boosting the power output from a MINI engine by means of forced induction – either independently or in addition to any more traditional modifications that may have been already carried out – and both are employed as standard on particular MINI models. They are by fitting either a turbocharger, as used on the MINI One D, or a supercharger, as standard on the Cooper S. The difference between them is that a turbocharger is driven by the escaping exhaust gases, while a supercharger is a mechanically driven device (basically it's a mechanical compressor which is belt driven by the engine).

In a normally-aspirated fuel-injected engine, such as that fitted to the MINI One and Cooper, the cylinders are filled with air at normal air pressure. With forced induction more air is forced into the cylinders at a greater pressure than that of the surrounding atmosphere, and when this happens, together with the correct amount of additional fuel, the end result is a great deal more power.

Modifying the Cooper S supercharger

The supercharger fitted to the MINI Cooper S is a Roots blower design, and is a type of supercharger normally used in high-speed engines requiring relatively low supercharge pressures. The unit is an Eaton M 45, which is actually a cut down version of the M 62, a supercharger that was first fitted to Buick V6s. It's based on a design patented around 1865 by F M and P H Roots in America, and was used for a number of purposes, including ventilating mines. It's driven by the engine by means of a Poly V-belt.

Within the supercharger two rotary pistons, or lobes, working in opposite directions compress (or strictly speaking displace) the incoming air to a maximum overpressure of 0.8bar. The compression causes the air to heat up, and to help remove the additional heat the air is then passed through an intercooler (which is supplied with cooling air from the air scoop on the S's bonnet) before entering the combustion chambers. Forced induction produced in this way provides a significant increase in engine power as combustion occurs.

Supercharged power units can be prone to engine knock or pre-ignition but this problem is overcome on the Cooper S engine by reducing the compression ratio to 8.3:1 (from 10.6:1). An electronic system, called Active Knock Control also monitors the combustion process, allowing the engine to run smoothly on unleaded fuel with an octane rating of anything between 91 and 98. This allows the use of the same engine and supercharger set-up in all markets throughout the world regardless of the quality of the fuel available.

A supercharger and intercooler installation in such a small area as the space under the bonnet of the Cooper S is neat and, all things considered, standard performance is very respectable indeed. But, the engineering compromise for ultimate reliability in the hands of the average driver is good news for the tuner as it means that with modification there's plenty more performance to be extracted. Supercharger modification is key to performance increases on the Cooper S, and it's the first area to receive attention from Stage 1 tuning upwards, and it also plays a key part in the John Cooper Works conversions.

Modification is straightforward. Considerable gains can be made by changing the supercharger pulley for a pulley of smaller diameter. This causes the supercharger to spin faster and, therefore, increases the boost pressure. Two types of modified pulley are available – a press on type and a bolt on type. Reduced-diameter pulleys are available from a number of tuners, usually in two sizes according to the amount of increased supercharger boost required.

The pulleys described here are made by Alta, although most pulleys available from other sources are of similar size. Quality is a major consideration when buying tuning equipment of this nature, and the Alta pulleys are made from stainless steel, which will wear at a much lesser rate than those pulleys made of aluminium, particularly the ones made of low-grade aluminium. The first size of modified pulley, and the most commonly fitted, is the 15% reduction

in diameter. The installation of this size of pulley will increase the supercharger boost to 1bar.

The second size is a 19% reduction in pulley diameter, and this will increase supercharger boost to 1.2bar. However, increasing the supercharger boost pressure further increases the amount of heat produced, and for this reason this size of pulley is only recommended for fitting together with an uprated intercooler (see below). There are other considerations when reducing the supercharger pulley by this higher amount. In the opinion of some tuners, notably Mini Mania, reducing the pulley diameter to less than 85% of its original diameter, i.e. a reduction of over 15%, will spin the supercharger faster than the maximum recommended, and could endanger or certainly reduce the life of the supercharger. The angle of the supercharger belt is also changed a lot more with the 19% reduction pulley, and belt life will be reduced accordingly.

When tuning any engine to high levels, some longevity and reliability is quite often compromised, this is one of the penalties. In a competition car, where the engine is regularly rebuilt and isn't normally expected to cover high mileages, this is less of a problem, but it's something to consider with a road car before undertaking the 19% mod.

When the supercharger pulley is changed for a smaller pulley, the ECU should be reprogrammed accordingly. Failure to do this can cause the engine to run lean.

Pulley removal
Changing the supercharger pulley is a job that can be undertaken at home, although it's likely that most owners will entrust the work to a specialist tuner who has experience of the mod. For those wanting to undertake the work at home a special tool made by Alta, and also by Amd, is required to remove the pulley, and this can be bought from a number of specialists. The pulley is fitted on incredibly tightly, and removal without the tool is simply not an option. The puller clamps around the entire belt surface of the supercharger pulley, applying force and clamping power ensuring that no damage will occur to the factory pulley or the supercharger. The stainless steel handle bolts solidly to the body of the pulley to allow the user to hold the pulley in place while extracting it from the supercharger. The puller is made of heat-treated hardened steel.

Supercharger drive belt
When the standard supercharger pulley is changed for a smaller pulley it's necessary to change the drive belt for a reduced diameter belt. Smaller belts are normally sold together with the smaller pulleys, and replacements are

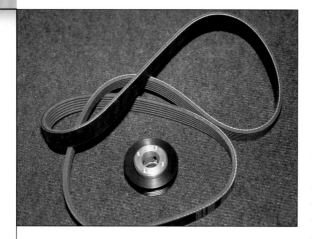

Reduced diameter pulley requires a different drive belt.

readily available from virtually all new MINI specialists.

Changing the supercharger

There's a limit to the amount of extra power that can be extracted by modifying the standard fitment supercharger. Further power gains can be achieved by fitting a different supercharger in the form of a Rotrex – this is being developed by Amd. The Rotrex supercharger is designed along the lines of a turbocharger and is in effect a 'driven turbo'. With this unit and suitable other engine modifications, power levels in excess of 300bhp are easily possible. The Rotrex supercharger requires an electric water pump to be fitted with a special flange to fit the cylinder block.

The intercooler

As mentioned earlier, the compressed air leaving the supercharger to enter the engine is hotter than the air from the atmosphere

The Cooper S intercooler.

entering the supercharger. This is mainly because compressing gases creates heat, also the supercharger is warmed by heat from the engine. To compensate for the additional heat that is generated, the Cooper S is fitted with an intercooler which cools the air entering the engine. Reducing the supercharged air intake temperature with an intercooler is beneficial for three reasons. First, it increases the density of the intake charge, resulting in more powerful combustion and creating more power. Second, there's a reduced need for the ECU to retard the ignition timing and increase the amount of fuel delivered. Third, reducing the general engine operating temperature will increase the life of the engine.

The standard intercooler is a small air-to-air unit of Behr design. It works well with the engine in standard form and is also capable of coping with some additional engine tuning. On the downside, the intercooler is fitted in a confined space at the top of the engine where temperatures are high. Also the air intake scoop in the bonnet is quite small and, therefore, limits the airflow into the supercharger, plus the exit path for the cooling air is restricted because of the engine components and the general lack of space in the engine compartment.

All this adds up to the fact that when the hot air from the supercharger passes through the intercooler, a considerable amount of heat is present in the air, and this heat enters the combustion chambers. Hot air expands and the oxygen content is reduced, resulting in a leaner mixture which only makes matters worse by further increasing combustion temperatures. This increases the possibility of pre-ignition, the ECU will detect the high exhaust gas temperature and will increase the fuel delivery and retard the ignition timing to bring the temperature down. This reduces the engine's power output and is very noticeable when a Cooper S is run on a rolling road with insufficient cool air being forced over the bonnet. This is a problem found with many rolling roads. The power output level does drop quite alarmingly, even on a standard car.

Generally, when the supercharger is modified, the boost level of the supercharger

increases and so does the level of heat generated. The MINI Cooper S's standard level of supercharger boost is about 0.8bar, and if a first stage smaller diameter supercharger pulley is installed, the boost level is increased to about 1bar and the result is that the amount of heat generated is further increased. The effect discussed above then becomes worse.

A quick and very cheap improvement, recommended by Mini Mania, which will assist the problem in a small way is to move the front number plate up to allow maximum airflow through the lower grille in the bumper.

Upgrading the intercooler

Under perfect conditions an air-to-air intercooler would have a high volume of airflow across the cooling elements, with a quick and unrestricted path out for the warmed air which has passed through. It would also be sited away from heat sources, such as the engine and the exhaust manifold. The most efficient air-to-air intercoolers are often mounted at the front of the car to ensure that maximum airflow is received to lower the temperature of the air into the supercharger by the maximum possible amount when the car is moving. With this in mind, a front-mounted intercooler system was under development by Owen Developments. Prototype intercoolers were produced and extensively tested by Mini Speed.

Unfortunately, there were problems with the set-up on the Cooper S because installation is very difficult in the very restricted space

between the bumper and the radiator. Also, a large amount of tubing is required which can result in a pressure drop in the charge air before it reaches the supercharger.

There are, however, several ways that have successfully been developed of upgrading the intercooler system. The first and simplest (and the cheapest) is to fit an improved air scoop into the intercooler in the form of an Alta Intercooler Air Diverter. This powder-coat-finished diverter replaces the standard fit factory unit with a more efficient design to increase flow through the intercooler. It's both taller and wider than the factory unit, thus forcing a larger volume of cool air over the intercooler surface. This increase in airflow helps to lower the air intake temperatures. It's worth noting here that, according to research carried out by Mini Mania, for every 10°F reduction of the incoming charge air temperature, the MINI produces 1% more power.

The next step is to fit an increased capacity intercooler unit in the standard position on top of the supercharger. A larger intercooler, such as the Alta top mount Intercooler, provides a 40% increase in cooling area and has the added advantage of not requiring any modifications to the car or supercharger in order to fit it. The Alta intercooler also seals to the underside of the bonnet and doesn't block the bonnet scoop. The intercooler kit includes the aforementioned air diverter and is considered by a number of specialist MINI tuners to be the best intercooler on the market.

This intercooler is also available with a water spray kit to further aid cooling and further increase efficiency.

Another good intercooler upgrade is produced by GRS Motorsport and is available from MED. The GRS intercooler has a specially designed diffuser. The core is the same thickness as the original to allow maximum airflow from the bonnet scoop, but there's a greater surface area to improve cooling. The end tanks have been designed to ensure a ram air effect through the core to achieve maximum cooling. Box design end tanks, with sharp edges don't work as well as the tapered end tanks of the GRS cooler. When the GRS Motorsport intercooler was tested on the rolling road, temperatures rose to no more than 38° at all times at 13–14psi, enabling maximum power to be achieved even in hot weather.

Water to air intercooler

A water spray kit will help to lower the intercooler temperature, but further exploitation of the idea of using water as a coolant and an alternative solution to a larger air-to-air intercooler (with or without a water spray) is to fit a full 'water-to-air' intercooler (available from Mini Mania). As the name suggests, this intercooler uses water as the cooling medium, instead of airflow. The major advantage of using water as a cooling medium is that there's a 14-fold greater heat transfer coefficient between aluminium and water than between aluminium and air. Also, cooling with water largely overcomes the problems of restricted cooling airflow both into the engine compartment and out once the air has passed over the intercooler. Water provides maximum cooling of the induction charge and keeps temperatures nearly constant. Heat from the intercooler is moved to an exchanger, or radiator, in front of the engine-cooling radiator, where it's dissipated to the atmosphere even when the cooling fan is off. Many water-to-air intercoolers that are available for other vehicles work by adding a water jacket over the air-to-air intercooler. These units perform adequately, but the design used by the Mini Mania Ultrik intercooler is 20% more efficient than water jacket-style intercoolers. The finned exterior on the cooler core creates a larger surface area compared to that of traditional 'radiator' style coolers, offering unparalleled heat transfer with minimal pressure drop.

The Ultrik water-to-air intercooler has continuously-flowing coolant, which overcomes the problem of heat soak, this is particularly useful in a road car, which frequently has to stop in traffic. When the car stops, so does the airflow over an air-to-air intercooler, and said

Larger intercooler will improve cooling and boost power.

There's room under the bonnet of the Cooper S for modified intercoolers … just.

Far left: The Ultrik water-cooled intercooler from Mini Mania.

Left: The Ultrik system uses a small radiator to cool the water.

intercooler absorbs heat rising from the engine and transfers the heat to the induction charge. When the car moves off again the performance will be poor due to 'corrective' action by the ECU, until fresh air entering through the bonnet scoop cools down the intercooler, and therefore the induction charge, returning things to normal.

The Ultrik cooler usually drops induction charge temperatures to within 15°F of the ambient air. It keeps temperatures at levels at which the engine management system can adjust fuelling and timing to achieve maximum power. Mini Mania say that there's up to a 15% power gain when using the water-cooled intercooler.

Another advantage of the Ultrik water-to-air intercooler is that it's a straightforward and very neat bolt-on installation that fits directly into the standard intercooler position location within the engine bay. The water radiator fits at the front of the engine bay using existing mounting points.

CryO$_2$ System

An alternative to using water as a cooling medium for the intercooler is to fit the CryO$_2$ system. A completely different idea which retains an air-to-air intercooler, the CryO$_2$ uses the cryogenic properties of CO$_2$ to dramatically lower the temperature of the intercooler cooling fins and therefore the induction charge. The CryO$_2$ system uses a bottle of compressed CO$_2$ and a sprayer, which mounts directly on top of the intercooler, venting liquid CO$_2$ onto the cooling fins and lowering the induction charge temperature by up to 60%. This improves the performance of the standard intercooler by up to 50%.

MINI One and Cooper

There are actually very few internal differences between the normally-aspirated One and Cooper engines and the supercharged Cooper S engine, so it would seem that a quick way to boost the performance of the normally-aspirated cars would simply be to bolt on a

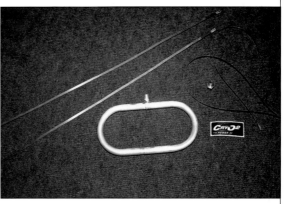

Far left: Ultimate intercooler cooling, the CryO$_2$ bottle ...

Left: ... and spray kit.

Cooper S supercharger and carry out any reprogramming of the ECU accordingly. But those 'very few' engine differences were included in the design of the Cooper S unit to cope with the extra mechanical loads placed on the engine by the supercharger. For example, the bottom end of the Cooper S engine is strengthened with larger diameter crankshaft journals and upgraded connecting rods. Because of these differences it isn't practical to fit a supercharger to the normally-aspirated engines. The easiest way to achieve supercharger performance is to sell the car and buy a Cooper S.

It is, however, possible to fit a turbocharger to the normally-aspirated petrol MINI engines. Kits are available for this and the subject is covered in the following section.

Turbocharging

Turbocharging differs from supercharging in that the turbine is driven by the gases collected in the exhaust manifold. Attached to the same shaft as the exhaust turbine, and therefore rotating at the same speed, but in a totally separate chamber within the turbo, is the inlet turbine. As the accelerator is pressed down, the engine sucks in more air/fuel mixture in exactly the same way as a normally-aspirated engine. As more exhaust is produced so the exhaust turbine spins faster and drives the inlet turbine at the same rate, forcing the air/fuel mixture into the cylinders under pressure. This produces the extra power as the engine doesn't have to

work so hard to suck in the air/fuel mix, and as the mixture is supplied under pressure it enters the engine much faster. Because exhaust has to be produced first to spin the turbo there's no boost at idle or low throttle openings, and it's why turbocharged cars sometimes suffer from turbo lag; that is the delay in the power coming through. The principle of operation is the same with a supercharger, it's just that a supercharger is engine driven rather than exhaust gas driven. The advantages of fitting a turbocharger are higher torque, which is good for acceleration from low speeds, lower exhaust noise and improved emissions, and in theory better fuel economy. The latter is rarely true in practice as in most cases the additional power is used most of the time, meaning that most turbocharged engines use more fuel than naturally-aspirated ones. In the case of the MINI the performance gains are certainly worthwhile.

The MINI One D turbocharger

The MINI One D, like the majority of modern diesel engines, is fitted with a turbocharger as standard. The One D turbo runs at speeds of up to 225,000rpm and compresses the incoming air to an overpressure of 1.2bar. Performance of this engine is further boosted by the standard fitment of an intercooler located next to the engine radiator; this receives its air supply through the radiator grille. One D engine modifications are limited to ECU, air filter and exhaust upgrades, and no modifications have been developed to upgrade the turbo. As it's designed for the Toyota derived diesel engine it isn't possible to fit the One D turbo to petrol-engined MINI models.

Turbocharging the petrol MINI One and Cooper

It's possible to considerably boost the output of the MINI One and Cooper by fitting a turbocharger, and with the correct turbo it's a fairly straightforward conversion.

Mini Mania were the first to offer a turbo conversion for the MINI Cooper. Developed by Cooper Turbo Research and Development Inc. in the United States, the complete kit is a bolt-on part, which requires no major modifications to the rest of the engine or the car. The turbo

An AmD development turbocharger for the MINI One and Cooper.

A cutaway turbocharger of the type suitable for fitting to the MINI. This was produced by Owen Developments.

kit produced 200bhp when bolted on to an otherwise completely standard 115bhp MINI Cooper. The Mini Mania kit is available internationally. In the UK, Amd also have a turbocharger kit for the MINI under development at the time of writing, which is likely to produce similar power figures to the Mini Mania kit. In general, a turbocharged engine will require a lower compression ratio than that of the equivalent naturally-aspirated engine. Therefore, converting a non-turbo engine such as the MINI's 1.6-litre unit, in many cases will involve a complete stripdown and rebuild using different (usually deeper dished) pistons or modifications to the cylinder head combustion chambers to achieve the lower ratio. All of these major modifications have been avoided on the MINI turbo kit by using a low blow turbo, i.e. keeping the turbo boost pressure down to only 6–8psi.

Turbocharging the MINI Cooper S

The MINI Cooper S is fitted with a supercharger as standard. There's probably little benefit in changing from a supercharger to a turbocharger, and as far as it's possible to tell this has never been attempted. However, turbocharging is relevant to the Pentagon-engined Cooper S as it's possible to retain the existing supercharger and fit a turbocharger as well. The limit in power terms that is reasonably possible with a supercharged only Cooper S engine employing the methods described in this book is realistically in the 260–270bhp region. Add a turbocharger in addition to the supercharger and this figure rises to 300bhp. One such conversion has been carried out in the USA by Mini Madness. The twin charging system uses a Garrett T28 turbocharger. Modification to the manifolding and inlet tubing is required, some of it being fairly complex, but the system is still essentially a bolt-on upgrade. Fuelling needs to be increased to match the larger volume of air being forced into the engine, and the cylinder head also requires modification to improve flow. Larger valves are needed, plus an uprated camshaft – the Mini Madness conversion uses a Schrick

The MINI turbo requires a special exhaust manifold.

The turbo bolts to the manifold. There's just room to house it in the MINI engine compartment.

cam. Larger fuel injectors are also employed. Exhaust manifolding includes a three-inch diameter downpipe and is specially tailored to the conversion, both to take account of the turbocharger and to improve flow characteristics. Clutch, flywheel, gearbox and differential upgrades, together with suspension and brake upgrades, are an absolute requirement at this level of engine power output.

The PSA Cooper S turbo engine
At the time of writing, all petrol-engined MINIs were fitted with the BMW and Chrysler developed Pentagon engine. It's worth noting in this chapter that turbocharging and the Cooper S will become far more widespread, as future Cooper Ss are to be fitted with a brand new turbocharged 1.6-litre petrol engine developed by BMW and PSA Peugeot Citroën.

The new 4-cylinder engine will be equipped with the latest type twinscroll turbocharger, a direct injection non-turbo version of the same engine will power the other MINIs in the range, plus some cars manufactured by PSA Peugeot Citroën. The engines are manufactured in the PSA factory at Douvrin in France. Early reports from tuners suggest that the bottom end of the engine isn't as robust as that of the Pentagon unit and this will restrict the ultimate power available. However, a number of tuning packages are likely to be available.

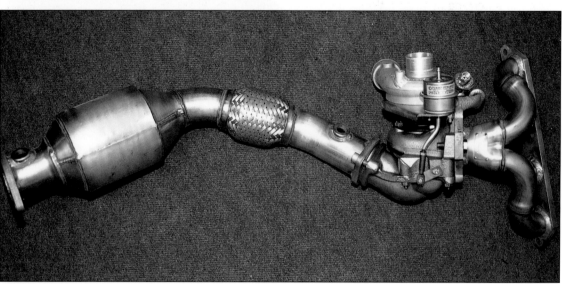

The full kit, including the catalytic converter and downpipe.

nitrous oxide injection

Another method that can be used to significantly boost power output is nitrous oxide (N_2O) injection. N_2O systems, which create large amounts of torque by allowing the engine to burn more fuel at a lower rpm range than normal, can be fitted to all petrol-engined MINIs, but they're mostly found on Cooper S models.

The power an engine produces from the fuel it burns relates directly to the amount of oxygen it can draw in. Normally this comes from air, but by injecting the gas nitrous oxide into the combustion process a boost of oxygen can be achieved. This comes from the engine's combustion temperature being more than enough to break the bond between N_2O's atoms, and thereby free up its oxygen. (Each molecule of nitrous oxide consists of 2 atoms of nitrogen and 1 atom of oxygen, and at 565°F the bond breaks down.) Once it has been separated from the nitrogen, the additional oxygen speeds the combustion of the additional fuel which is simultaneously introduced. At the same time the separated nitrogen acts as a buffer against detonation, damping down some of the increased mechanical load on the engine.

So, since it's oxygen we want, why not inject neat O_2? The answer lies largely in the last sentence of the above paragraph. Although nitrogen doesn't aid combustion, it does play its part in absorbing heat, and it's not possible to add much pure oxygen before the additional heat starts to cause problems. Another downside to pure oxygen is that it remains as a gas when compressed, so storage bottles are much larger – a particular disadvantage in a MINI. To put it simply, by using nitrous oxide we can get more oxygen atoms in the engine and have useful extra nitrogen as well. Nitrous can add a lot more power before the heat level becomes uncontrollable. Incidentally, contrary to popular belief, N_2O isn't in itself flammable.

To run any nitrous system successfully and safely, it's necessary to introduce precise amounts of additional fuel at the same time as the correct amount of nitrous oxide. All of the extra oxygen provided by the nitrous oxide must have fuel with which to burn or serious engine damage is likely to occur. So, more oxygen requires more petrol, and therefore a petrol solenoid is fitted as well as a nitrous solenoid. In this way N_2O is injected into the manifold together with petrol rather than on its own.

Large power increases achieved by using nitrous oxide can increase the chance of detonation or pre-ignition. The chemically correct nitrous to petrol ratio is 9.649:1. If a nitrous-injected engine is allowed to run on a weak mixture the engine can be destroyed in a matter of seconds. Fuelling must be maintained at the correct ratio or temperatures will rise rapidly. All nitrous systems come with rich fuel jetting; the extra fuel helps to keep down the heat and raises the detonation limit. Systems such as the M7 Venom, available from Mini Mania, will immediately shut off the nitrous flow if the Venom system detects that the engine is running lean.

We have already mentioned that engines produce more power when the induction air is cooler. Cooler intake air is denser and contains more oxygen atoms, this allows more fuel to be burned and produces more power. A 10° drop in temperature can add 1 to 1.5% power to an engine. Nitrous oxide boils at –129°F and it will begin to boil as soon as it's injected. This can cause an 80° or so drop in manifold air temperature. This cooling effect also helps in preventing detonation. When the amount of nitrous and additional fuel is controlled correctly, the engine can safely and reliably generate quite exceptional power increases.

There are several nitrous systems on the market tailored to the MINI. Most provide more than one level of power increase; the lower power boost systems are quickly and cheaply upgradeable to higher power output levels. Nitrous kits from Wizards of Nos in Doncaster, South Yorkshire, for example, come in 25, 50, 75 and 100bhp versions. The power level is controlled by metering jets installed in the solenoid outlets/jet holders. To change the power output, all you need to do is install the appropriate set of jets. Many manufacturers will only sell you a 25bhp kit to begin with. Once this has been fitted, and the results reported back to them, they will consider selling the parts to increase the power boost to 50bhp.

With power increases of 50bhp and above, the ignition timing will need to be retarded; or better still, a Powamax progressive controller can be fitted which will allow a greater amount of usable power to be released.

Nitrous components

The largest component in a nitrous kit is the cylinder containing pressurised liquid N_2O. The cylinder should be fitted in as cool a place as possible in the car. This is because it's important to keep the nitrous in liquid form as long as possible in order to gain maximum power. The cylinder is connected by a hose to a solenoid valve. This hose should be as short as possible and run along the coolest possible path, again to delay vaporisation. The solenoid valve is mounted under the bonnet, and is engaged and disengaged via a throttle switch. A T-piece fitted into the fuel line feeds fuel to another solenoid which is also activated by the same throttle switch. Both the nitrous and fuel solenoids should be mounted in the coolest spot under the bonnet, while trying to maintain the shortest output line length – not easy in a MINI, particularly a Cooper S. The nitrous oxide and fuel that is to be delivered to the engine's air inlet is conveyed via two delivery lines to an injector mounted in the inlet manifold, and the system is switched on and off by means of a dashboard mounted switch.

The big advantage of nitrous is that it runs at full throttle only, so the car can be driven normally even when the system is switched on. The additional power comes in at any rpm

A nitrous oxide bottle ...

when the throttle is floored, in a similar fashion to the way a kickdown operates on a car with automatic transmission.

Points to note

It's important to ensure that a nitrous system is never operated with an empty nitrous bottle. Operating without N_2O flowing through will cause the solenoid to overheat and fail.

Nitrous works very well on both totally standard and tuned MINIs, and just about anything that is normally done to improve the performance of the engine can be done when nitrous is installed. Correct installation is vital, though. More than one MINI engine has been destroyed by a nitrous system, which is why most owners wanting to fit nitrous opt for having the work carried out by a qualified company.

Before fitting nitrous it's advisable to speak to your insurance company. This is the case with any modification, of course, but it's particularly important when planning to have a nitrous system installed as most insurance companies aren't very enthusiastic about it!

... and the rest of the components required for installing an N_2O system.

the cylinder head

One of the most critical aspects of the whole combustion process is the design of the cylinder head – the combustion chamber in particular, as well as the inlet and exhaust ports. For maximum power the engine must run at the highest possible compression ratio that can be used without knocking, and its propensity to knock is very dependent upon the anti-knock rating, or octane number, of the fuel being used. The Mini One and Cooper have a 10.6:1 compression ratio, and this is normally about as high as can safely be run, bearing in mind that in some countries the octane rating of fuel is very low. Without electronic engine management it's unlikely that a compression ratio this high could be used. The Cooper S has a compression ratio of 8.3:1; it's lower because supercharged engines run with much lower compression ratios than normally-aspirated engines.

Modifying the cylinder head

In the past, cylinder head modification was probably the most important part of extracting a higher level of performance from a standard production engine. Modifying the head on current engines, the MINI petrol range included, still plays an important part in upgrading performance, but the results of modification won't provide as dramatic a power increase as was seen on older design engines, notably on the A Series engine fitted to all classic Minis. The new MINI engine head is, like most modern designs, reasonably efficient in standard form; proof of this is the standard power output of the supercharged Cooper S engine. Big power increases can be achieved with the head in standard form, but once the power output of the S goes significantly over the 200bhp mark, head modification is an essential part of taking power levels higher.

There are two main stages of modification of a MINI cylinder head. Modified cylinder heads are available off the shelf from several suppliers. Like most things, some are better than others, so it's essential to buy from a reputable supplier; preferably one which comes with a

The MINI cylinder head showing the combustion chambers.

The head from above showing the spark plug tubes.

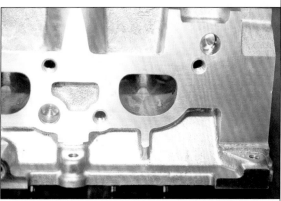

The porting on the standard head.

There's room for improvement in the standard ports.

Right: Cutaway showing the internal port design 1.

Far right: Cutaway showing internal port design 2.

Port marked for modification.

Modifying a MINI cylinder head in the head shop at MED Engineering.

Close up on the modification work.

recommendation. MINI head modification involves gas-flowing the head to minimise obstruction of the fuel/air mix both entering and leaving the combustion chamber. On good-quality heads, such as those from MED Engineering, the inlet and exhaust ports are reshaped and enlarged quite extensively, and they're also polished where appropriate to smooth the flow of the gases. Also the shape of the combustion chamber is altered, and quite a lot of work is carried out, particularly around the spark plug area, where there's a lot of excess material which retains heat when the engine is running. Most of the first stage heads are fully ported and polished, but they retain the standard fitment inlet and exhaust valves. This level of modification, as used on the JCW Works Coopers, produces increased power and provides a useful upgraded road-specification head. However, some of the stage 1 heads available from independent specialists are modified to a higher degree than the JCW heads.

More power can be obtained with the next stage up, such as those supplied by MED which have a lot more work carried out on the ports, plus they're fitted with larger inlet and exhaust valves. These big-valve heads are available from numerous suppliers worldwide. The MED heads are fitted with superior quality valves and guides (detailed more fully below). This level of modified head is normally fitted at higher levels of tune, and will work well with intercooler upgrades and an upgraded camshaft. Modified heads are available for the One/Cooper and the Cooper S. A well-modified head can add as much as 20–30bhp to the power output of an engine.

The rocker gear

The standard valve operating equipment fitted to the MINI is sufficiently strong and light for all levels of tune, and upgrades are neither considered necessary by MINI tuners nor currently available.

Valves

Again, the standard valves are of good quality and suitable for levels of tune that don't require the fitting of larger valves. Larger valves are available and are fitted as standard to highly modified heads from the specialist suppliers. They can also be fitted to an existing head along with suitable gasflowing work by a qualified machine shop. The best ones are plasma nitrided valves, as fitted to all big-valve heads produced by MED Engineering. The MED larger valve sizes are 31.5mm inlet and 24.5mm exhaust. MED valves are single cotter valves, as opposed to the three-cotter type fitted as standard. When these are fitted, upgraded collets and caps (also supplied by MED) must be used.

Valve springs

The standard valve springs are strong enough for the larger valves and performance camshafts that are currently available, and don't need to be replaced if they're in good condition.

Valve guides

The same is true of the valve guides. The standard fitment guides haven't shown any tendency to wear excessively and are fully up to coping with tuning. They should, however, be inspected as and when cylinder head overhaul

MED larger valves.

MED uprated valve springs.

MED upgraded spring caps.

the camshaft

The MINI petrol engine has a single overhead camshaft, i.e. a single camshaft opens both the inlet and exhaust valves. It's located in the cylinder head and is driven by a timing chain. Once tuning of the engine has reached a certain level, a change to an uprated camshaft is required before further tuning can be effectively undertaken. MINI camshafts have 12 cams, three for each cylinder. Two cam lobes operate two rocker arms for the two inlet valves per cylinder and another lobe operates a dual rocker arm to open the two exhaust valves per cylinder. By altering the point at which the valves open and close, and also the degree to which they open, it's possible to increase the performance of the engine.

Upgrading the camshaft

As a general rule, fitting a hotter camshaft will make an engine less smooth, particularly at idle; the hotter the cam the worse the situation becomes. MINI upgrade camshafts are relatively mild, and most fall into the 'fast road' bracket rather than 'rally' or 'full race', meaning that the effect on the engine's smoothness at idle, and the ability to pull away smoothly at low revs, is largely unaffected. Fitting a very high lift cam into a MINI is, at the current time, not possible because of the design of the cylinder head and the positioning of the spark plug tubes. A cam with high-lift lobes will foul the tubes. However, very good performance increases can be obtained from the cams that are available.

Valve collets, standard on right and MED upgraded on the left.

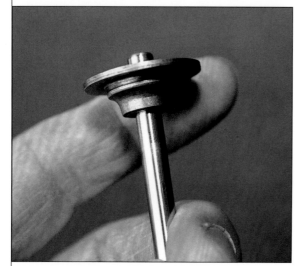

MED upgrade valve caps and collets on valve.

Far right: The proximity of the camshaft lobes to the spark plug tubes in this picture demonstrates the limitations in height of camshaft lobes and therefore cam lift.

becomes necessary, or if excessive oil consumption is a problem. When better-quality valves are fitted, such as the larger valves made specially for MED, silicon bronze guides to suit the valves should be fitted. These are fitted to all MED big-valve performance cylinder heads.

The cylinder head gasket

The cylinder head gasket is generally reliable, although some leakage has been experienced in a few cases on tuned MINIs, and even in a few cases on the standard car. From a tuning point of view, consider 300bhp to be about the upper limit that the standard head gasket will cope with. No upgrade gaskets are currently available.

Performance fast road camshafts, giving increased lift and duration, are available from a number of suppliers, such as MED, Mini Speed, Mini Spares and Mini Mania. Camshafts are available for both the normally-aspirated petrol-engined MINIs and the supercharged S. The uprated cams are manufactured by specialist suppliers, such as Piper, Schrick and Kent, and most are supplied manufactured from blanks, i.e. from brand new uncut shafts and not on an exchange basis where an existing camshaft is reprofiled. The majority of these cams are suitable for both road and competition use.

Specialist camshaft companies, like Kent Cams, can create any profile from the vast 'library' of available profiles. This is part of the selection of profiles available from Kent.

The Piper MINI fast road cam

The Piper 270 MINI cam is used by a number of independent tuners, particularly in the UK. The specification of the cam is as follows:

Cam	Piper MINBP270
Power band	1,500–6,500rpm
Inlet duration	256°
Exhaust duration	248°
Inlet valve lift	.350in (9.14mm)
Exhaust valve lift	.350in (8.89mm)
Inlet timing	16 open, 60 close
Exhaust timing	56 open, 12 close
Full lift	112° after TDC inlet
	112° before TDC exhaust

Valve lifts assume a rocker ratio of 1.645:1 inlet and 1.4:1 exhaust.
Hydraulic tappets are fitted to the MINI.

Cams are ground from new blanks.

A MINI upgraded camshaft of the type available from Piper or Kent.

An alternative performance camshaft from Schrick.

Another reputable cam is the Schrick. As a comparison, the timing figures supplied by Schrick for the Cooper S shaft are as follows:

Inlet valve lift	9.5mm
Exhaust valve lift	9.0mm
Inlet duration	264°
Exhaust duration	272°
Timing	114°

The MINI timing chain.

The timing chain at the lower (crankshaft) end.

Performance camshaft terminology

Lift. Lift is either the lift provided by the cam lobe, i.e. the difference between the lowest and highest points of the lobe, or valve lift; valve lift is the cam lift multiplied by the rocker ratio to give the amount of valve opening. The racier the cam the higher the lift.

Duration. Duration is the number of degrees of crankshaft rotation that the valve is off its seat. To calculate inlet duration, the inlet timing numbers should be added together plus 180°. For the MINI cam this is 16 + 60 = 76 +180° = 256°.

Overlap. Overlap is the number of degrees of crankshaft rotation that the inlet and exhaust valves are open at the same time. Overlap is calculated by adding the opening inlet degree figure to the closing figure of the exhaust. For the Piper cam above, this is 16 + 12 giving 28°. The higher the number, the greater the overlap and the hotter the cam.

Cam Timing. Cam timing is the position of the camshaft relative to the crankshaft. In the case of inlet timing this is after top dead centre (after TDC), and for exhaust timing before top dead centre (before TDC). TDC is top dead centre of No. 1 piston. To calculate timing, take the inlet figures of 16/60, add them together and add 180. 16 + 60 = 76 +180 = 256. Then halve this number to get 128, and deduct the number of degrees before TDC that the valve started to open, i.e. 16. 128 − 16 = 112. The valve is correctly timed at 112° after TDC.

Valve Timing. Valve timing is the opening and closing position of the inlet and the exhaust valves in relation to the crankshaft, quoted as before and after TDC.

Camshaft drive

The camshaft drive on the MINI petrol engine is a crankshaft-driven roller timing chain. This is good news for longevity and reliability as timing chains rarely break, compared to the breakage frequency of cam belts and resulting serious engine damage. BMW converted back to chain drive many years ago and it's reassuring to see a chain employed on the MINI engine – it's also a Mini tradition. The standard chain is strong and reliable and no upgrade is available or needed.

blocks, cranks, rods, pistons, cooling and oil

All of the petrol engines fitted to MINIs have a 77mm bore and an 85.8mm stroke, the crankshaft having five main bearings. The MINI Cooper S internal engine design remains fundamentally the same as the One and Cooper, but the crankshaft, connecting rods, pistons, engine bearings and valves have all been uprated to cope with the increased thermal and mechanical loads produced by the supercharger. Additionally, a small oil cooler is fitted, plus there's splash oil cooling of the pistons to provide additional engine cooling and lubrication. Building a high-performance MINI engine is simpler than it is for many cars, and certainly considerably simpler than the old Mini ever was, because the bottom end of the engine doesn't need any modification; it's strong enough in standard form, even for most types of competition work.

The cylinder block

The cylinder block is made of cast iron, and also appears to be strong and wear resistant. At the time of writing, no oversize pistons were available as off-the-shelf items. In the event of excessive wear to the block after a high mileage or operation in less than ideal conditions, the only remedy is a replacement block, or boring and linering the block and fitting new standard sized pistons.

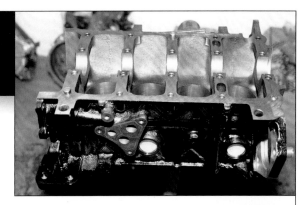

A MINI Cooper S engine block.

Main bearing with built in thrust washer.

The lower main bearing cap section of the block.

Far left: Torqueing down the main bearings.

Left: Rebored cylinder block.

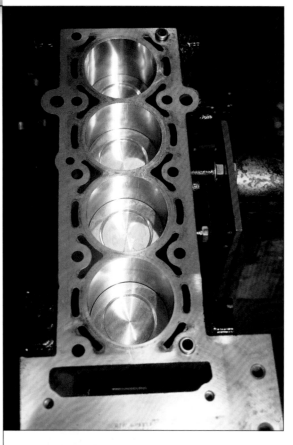

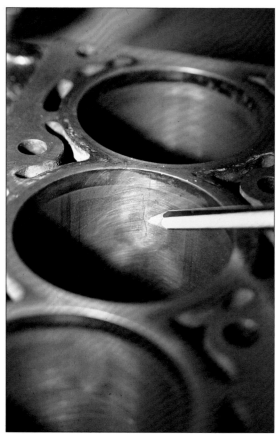

Right: Big bore block with pistons fitted.

Far right: This is where cracks can appear in the cylinder on big bore MINI engines.

Big bore engines

That said, it's possible to have pistons made to the required size by specialist companies such as J E Pistons, who will make small batches and one-off sets. A number of attempts to enlarge the capacity of the MINI engine have been made by overboring the block to 1800cc, and in some cases also stroking the crankshaft. Overboring doesn't seem to work on this engine. For some reason, when it's bored out to a larger size the block has a tendency to crack. Large bore engines are very expensive to produce and the power gain that is achieved by increasing the capacity of a MINI engine by approximately 200cc isn't considered by tuners to be worth the considerable effort and expense involved.

Mini Speed produced an 1800cc conversion, which was fitted to their development MINI, but this suffered from cracking of the block and was subsequently abandoned. The development car continues with a standard capacity, but still heavily modified, Cooper S engine.

The Chrysler Pentagon engine is also fitted to the Chrysler Neon in 2.0-litre form; so, in theory, an engine swap to the 2.0-litre unit would seem to be the sensible way to gain extra capacity. However, this has been investigated by MINI tuners such as Mini Speed and the conclusion is that there are too many differences in the engine units to make this a viable proposition.

The crankshaft

The crankshaft is a five main bearing unit. It's very strong in standard form and no strengthening mods are required. If the engine is dismantled for any reason it's worthwhile having the crank balanced and also polished if any marks are present; the latter is only likely to be the case with high mileage engines. MINI cranks can be reground if wear is present after a high mileage, one undersize is possible, this being 0.25mm. The crank thrust washers are built into the centre main bearing. Gaining

Cooper S crankshaft.

Far left: Close up of crank journals. This is a standard repolished crank.

Left: Lowering the crank into a bored out engine block.

extra capacity by lengthening the stroke isn't possible using the standard crank. as it was by using certain component combinations on the original Mini. Longer stroke cranks have to be specially made, and this option was being tried by Cool New, but whether the outcome of the operation was successful is unknown as the company closed down. MED also investigated the idea but came to the conclusion that, as one-off long-stroke cranks are exceptionally expensive, they're unlikely to play a part in gaining greater performance from the MINI engine.

A lightened crankshaft bottom pulley produced by Alta is available and provides a useful weight reduction. The original weighs 3.2kg, while the lightened bottom pulley weighs in at only 417g! It looks good too! The pulley is interference fit and a special puller is required to remove it. The surface of the crank should be lightly cleaned with fine emery cloth before fitting the new pulley.

Lightweight performance crank pulley fitted to a Mini Speed performance engine.

MINI rods are of the 'broken' variety, meaning that the caps aren't under any circumstances interchangeable.

Right: The little end of the rods needs minor machining when some modified pistons are fitted.

Far right: ARP upgraded rod bolts.

Connecting rods

The standard con rods are fully up to performance increases. The big ends are one piece and broken at the big end, making it impossible to fit the wrong cap to a rod. The rod bolts can be upgraded by fitting high-quality ARP rod bolts, which are suitable for both naturally-aspirated and supercharged engines. They're recommended for all high-output MINI engines.

Pistons

As already stated, oversize pistons aren't readily available. The only pistons available off-the-shelf are the standard items. These are capable of coping with very high engine outputs, even from the supercharged Cooper S engine. J E Pistons produced the pistons used in the Mini Speed high-capacity engine; they're of very high quality and are made to order.

Right: Modified performance piston, in this case from JE.

Far right: Gapping the rings before fitting upgraded pistons.

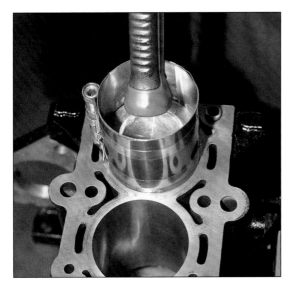

Far left: Fitting performance pistons to the block.

Left: J E piston installed in a block at Mini Speed.

The cooling system

The standard fitment radiator is of high capacity and suitable for all levels of tuning currently available. Silicon hoses can be used to replace the standard rubber components, and these will last longer as they're much less prone to deterioration from the chemical content of the antifreeze, the temperature variation and general ageing. They also look good, if you like coloured hoses. Further details on how to reduce engine temperatures on the Cooper S where high heat levels are a problem can be found in the supercharger section.

The oil system

The standard oil pump and oil system are suitable for all levels of tune in all MINI engine variations. Regular oil changes are essential for any engine, particularly when the performance is increased. Additional oil changes over and above the recommended change frequency are sometimes worthwhile on cars which cover a low annual mileage, or regularly only cover short journeys. Ensure that the oil used is the correct fully synthetic 5w/40 viscosity oil as approved by BMW for New MINI servicing.

If oil temperatures are likely to be a problem, or the engine is tuned to a high level, an oil cooler kit is available. The kit consists of an oil cooler radiator, two braided hoses and a block adapter plate, which accepts the braided hose ends and feeds directly into the cylinder block.

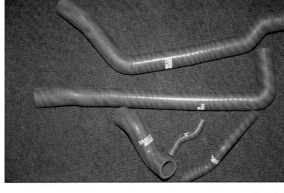

A set of performance silicon cooling system hoses.

The MINI oil pick-up pipe.

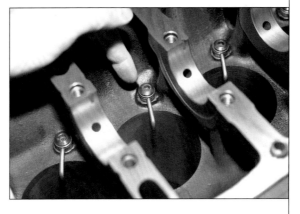

The lubrication system in the Cooper S block.

the exhaust system

The MINI exhaust system on all models consists of the manifold, which connects to the cylinder head, the catalytic converter (or cat), which forms part of the manifold, followed by the pipe and silencer, and last the tailpipe at the rear of the car. Engine performance is greatly affected by the speed at which the exhaust gases can escape from the cylinders through the exhaust system. The easier and faster they escape, the better the engine performance will be. Changing the standard equipment exhaust system on all the petrol-engined MINIs for one of the many higher-performance systems on the market makes a big improvement. That an upgraded exhaust features in all the car conversions, excluding pure remaps, is proof of this.

There are a number of exhaust upgrade options from several companies, including BMW, who offer sports exhaust systems for most MINI models, including the MINI One D. The BMW systems replace the silencers after the catalytic converter; they're made of stainless steel and produce a sportier exhaust note as well as improving rear end appearance. Complete systems, including upgraded exhaust manifolds and uprated catalytic converters, are available from specialist aftermarket companies. Earlier stage tuning usually involves replacing the exhaust system only, higher stage tuning means changing the manifold too.

Cat back systems

Fitting a performance exhaust from the catalytic converter backwards (usually referred to as a 'cat back' system) is a popular mod. It's the first

Right: The standard MINI One and Cooper exhaust system is quite restrictive.

Far right: The same is true of the Cooper S system ...

... the degree of restriction becoming more obvious when the system is removed from the car if the escape routing of the gases is anything to go by!

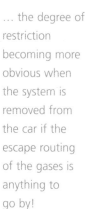

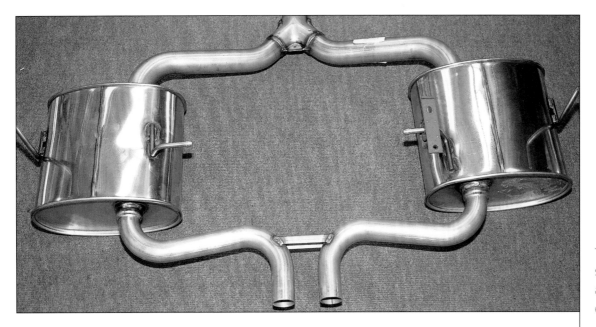

The upgraded system routing is a lot more direct.

step in improving the exhaust system and it's about the only engine performance mod that can be done on its own without the need for an ECU remap. Fitting a cat back system is quite straightforward and is something that can easily be undertaken at home without the need for specialised equipment.

The standard systems on both normally-aspirated MINIs and the Cooper S are surprisingly restrictive; this is particularly the case with the Cooper S. There are many aftermarket systems to choose from, and when selecting the system for your MINI it's important to choose one that not only looks good but performs well and has an exhaust note that suits your purposes. Noisy systems sound great when driving around locally, but they can become exceedingly tiresome on a long journey. Some systems available in the USA have the advantage of a silent tip to the exhaust system, which can be added to quieten it on long runs.

It's important to buy exhaust components from a company which has tested and

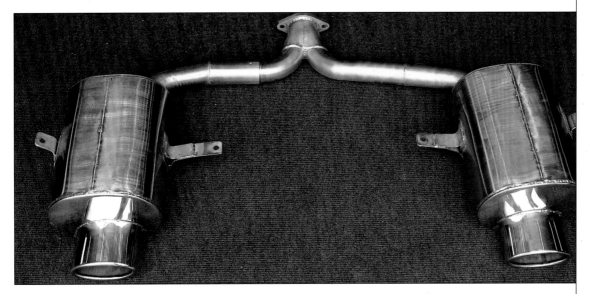

Twin side exit system pipework is even more straight through.

approved the systems that it offers for sale. Mini Speed, for instance, offer a good range to suit all budgetary, noise and appearance requirements and all have been tested by Mini Speed on their own development Cooper S. It's worth mentioning that during their tests Mini Speed found that one aftermarket exhaust system was so restrictive that it ended up melting a piston!

Amongst the systems available from Mini Speed is the Laser range, including the Laser stainless steel twin centre-exit exhaust for the MINI One and Cooper. This comes as a

complete single box system with twin round centre exit tailpipes, and a new rear skirt shaped to fit around the tailpipes – all fittings are supplied with the kit. A Laser stainless steel twin side-exit exhaust for MINI One & Cooper is also available. This comes as a complete system featuring twin round tailpipes exiting either side of the car. The rear skirt needs to have a slice taken out of it on the left-hand side to allow for fitment of the additional tailpipe. Again, all necessary fittings come with the kit. The tailpipes are 100mm in diameter. For the Cooper S there's a Laser twin duplex side-exit stainless steel exhaust system complete with twin silencers, a link pipe up to the catalytic converter flange, and twin duplex rear pipes.

Play Mini, well known in the Japanese market for a large range of classic Mini parts and accessories and also well known in the UK for original Mini exhausts, produce systems for the MINI One and Cooper consisting of a 3in slash-cut rear silencer, or TT-style rear silencer and a link pipe. These are high-quality exhaust systems, which sound really good, and are also extremely easy to fit. Made from stainless steel,

Different tail pipes are available on some upgrade systems.

Right: Twin centre upgrade tail pipes from Mini Mania.

Far right: Huge twin side exit pipes from Mini Mania.

Right: Slightly smaller diameter twin side exit pipes on the AmD development Cooper S are more in proportion with the car.

Far right: Huge single system on MINI Cooper.

they require a Play Mini link pipe to connect to the MINI's exhaust manifold flange. The link pipe for the Play Mini slash-cut and TT-style silencers is also made from stainless steel. Cooper S systems are also available. Two sports silencers are available for the Cooper S – a twin 72mm central pipe system or a four-outlet system. Often four pipes on a small car like the Mini will look overcrowded, but this system, reminiscent of the BMW E46 M3, does look very good. Again, it's extremely easy to fit, and is supplied as a complete system to bolt up to the manifold flange.

Stainless systems with a slash-cut tailpipe system for the One and Cooper, and a twin tailpipe system for the S are also produced by Scorpion.

One of the most popular exhaust systems, particularly with UK tuners, is the Milltek range. The Milltek is available as a side exit system for Mini One and Cooper with a 90mm round tailpipe, and with a special tailpipe – a round design with no inward roll. These are supplied complete with all fixtures and fittings. The Milltek stainless steel exhaust system for Cooper S features twin rounded-end tailpipes with a slash-cut and no inward roll. This system has been developed to produce the best exhaust note, and least resonance when the engine performance has been increased.

MINI One D
Milltek produce a side exit exhaust system for the MINI One diesel. This higher performance system comes complete with a turbo downpipe, two connecting pipes, a rear silencer and a 90mm round tailpipe. Performance is improved as well as the exhaust note.

Manifolds and catalytic converters
The catalytic converter forms part of the downpipe of the exhaust manifold. The standard catalyst is somewhat restrictive and there's a benefit in changing to a higher performance cat. A stainless steel high-performance exhaust manifold and catalyst upgrade is produced by Milltek. This is a four into one system with substantially lengthened primary pipes. It considerably improves the

outflow of the exhaust gases, and the cat is also much improved over standard. The improved cat contains a 250 cell per inch metal catalyst, which offers a 34% greater open area than the standard catalyst, and has the benefit of reducing back pressure. It's unaffected by prolonged exposure to the high temperatures of the exhaust system. The Milltek manifold and cat, when coupled to a Milltek exhaust system, will give an 18bhp power increase. This system is available from Mini Speed, Moss, and Birds – who also sell Hartge sports exhausts.

Play Mini produce a stainless steel tubular

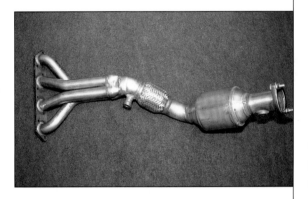

AmD upgraded exhaust manifold …

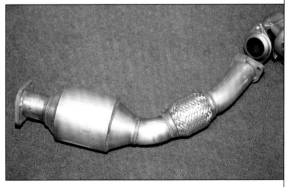

… with catalytic converter shown removed from the manifold.

Three different diameter manifolds from MED.

The different diameters of the pipes are clearly visible here – the centre smallest diameter pipe is the standard Cooper S fitment.

Far right: Mini Mania longer four into one manifold.

Right: Big upgraded sports catalytic converter from Mini Mania.

Right: Be sure to get the correct system for your MINI, the mountings vary on later models.

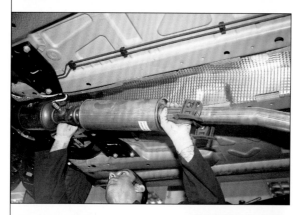

Below left: With many performance silencers the heat shielding will require some modification.

Far right: Careful alignment is essential when fitting a modified exhaust system.

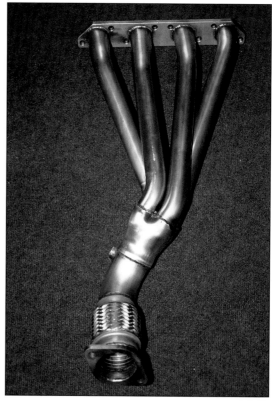

exhaust manifold, which includes a performance cat to fit all petrol MINI models. Mini Speed also produce their own stainless steel exhaust manifold and stainless steel performance exhaust manifold with high-flow catalyst.

Exhaust mountings

The exhaust mounting points vary according to model year on all models. Before purchasing an exhaust system from an aftermarket supplier, check to ensure that it's compatible with the model year of your MINI.

engine bay enhancements

For many owners of tuned MINIs (tuned road MINIs in particular) the appearance under the bonnet will be important. A highly tuned engine can often look very similar to the standard factory version, and a few engine bay enhancements can quickly correct this situation. The first requirement is cleanliness, and this can easily be achieved using one of the many available engine-cleaning products. On top of this there are a number of other improvements that can enhance the look of things. Some of them are purely cosmetic, others also have a function – a good example being the silicon cooling hose kit that can be obtained from a number of new MINI specialists.

Here are some examples of the many products on the market at the time of writing:

Silicon hose kit

MINI engines are fitted as standard with synthetic rubber cooling system hoses. Today's cooling hoses are much more long lived than those of a couple of decades ago, but over time they do deteriorate and eventually wear out. The hoses deteriorate from the inside out and this process is accelerated on a hard driven or highly tuned engine. Silicon hose kits are available to replace both radiator and heater system hoses, which not only improve the appearance of the engine bay, but will last a great deal longer as they're much less prone to internal deterioration than the standard equipment 'rubber' items. Silicon hose kits are available from most MINI specialists in blue, but

There are many cosmetic underbonnet improvements, such as chrome caps for virtually all tanks and fillers.

Painting on the intercooler cover is one way to individualise the engine in a Cooper S.

can also be obtained for the Cooper S in red and black from Mini Spares.

Intercooler cover

Some MINI owners paint their intercooler cover, but an alternative is to replace it with a carbon fibre version. The carbon cover is available from Mini Spares and is a direct replacement for the standard plastic cover.

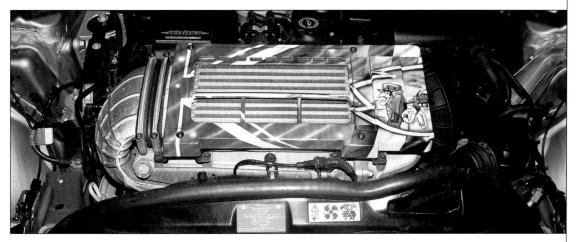

The possibilities here are endless.

Alloy replacements are available ...

One and Cooper and to upgrade the small cooler fitted to the Cooper S. The kit comes complete with an oil cooler radiator, two braided hoses and a block adapter plate, which accepts the braided hose ends and feeds directly into the block.

Oil catch tank
Oil catch tanks are available in both blue and red from Mini Speed.

Engine oil cap
An improved engine oil cap can be fitted over the factory item. The centre of the new cap cover is open to allow the factory wording to show through, and these are available from Mini Mania. Billet alloy caps are available from Moss, but these are replacement caps and don't show factory oil cap wording.

Aluminium expansion tank
Alloy expansion tanks are available to replace the standard plastic tanks, which have been known to split along the seam over time. Aluminium not only looks a great deal smarter, it's also unlikely to split and should last the life of the car without problems. Expansion tank splitting is a particular problem on pre 2004 model year MINIs, making this a particularly worthwhile upgrade on earlier cars.

Oil cooler kit
Oil cooler kits are available for fitting to the

Dip sticks
Billet alloy dipsticks with a Cooper or Cooper S logo are available from Moss. They are a direct replacement for the original stick. MINI logo dipsticks are available from Mini Spares in a variety of styles and colours.

... for all tanks including the expansion tank and the power steering reservoir.

Top left: Alloy pulleys improve the look of the engine and save weight too.

Top right: Strut braces are really a suspension mod, but many people fit them for purely aesthetic reasons.

Left: A number of designs are available from different specialists.

Left: Poly engine mounts add cosmetic appeal as well as stiffening things up.

Brake reservoir cap

To go hand in hand with the oil cover cap, and again from Mini Mania, is a brake fluid reservoir cap cover. As with the oil cover cap, the factory wording remains visible in the centre of the new cap cover. Alloy windscreen washer caps are also available.

Aluminium power steering reservoir kits

A two-piece power steering reservoir enhancement set comes with a cap to slip over the factory cap and a cover to fit over the top part of the reservoir tank. Alternatively a complete replacement alloy reservoir tank is available from specialists such as Mini Spares.

Nut covers

Nut covers are available for a number of exposed nuts in the engine bay. These include covers for the earth strap, the coil and the suspension struts. A cover is also available for the strut towers; this, however, will only fit MINIs fitted with sports suspension.

Air conditioning check valve covers

Two vented covers are available to fit over the air conditioning check valves.

Plug leads

A number of different plug leads are available in differing qualities from most MINI specialists. These enhance the overall appearance under the bonnet as well as improving performance; full details of some of the types available are given in the Electronic Tuning section.

Other items to consider

As well as the items listed there are other components which can be considered when customising the underbonnet area of a MINI. These include air filter kits and suspension strut braces, both of which are available in a number of different designs; also polyurethane engine mountings. Intercooler upgrades provide a different underbonnet look, and all these items are described in the chapters covering the primary function of the components.

When MINI engine tuning is carried out it is also important to consider upgrading the transmission. All clutches and gearboxes will cope with moderate stages of tuning, but when higher levels of power are planned, improvements to the transmission components become essential, even on the already better equipped Cooper S.

the clutch

All manual transmission MINIs are fitted with a maintenance-free hydraulically-operated clutch, and in standard form it's more than capable of coping with any tuning likely to be carried out on the One Diesel. In the case of the petrol-engined MINIs, the standard clutch is suitable for most road tuned engines, but for high levels of tune a clutch upgrade will be necessary. The Cooper S clutch is stronger than the One/Cooper clutch and capable of coping with quite high levels of tune before that upgrade becomes necessary. An illustration of this is that a competition paddle clutch was produced for BMW Motorsport by AP Braking for the JCW MINI Cooper Challenge, but this wasn't deemed necessary for the Cooper S Challenge.

Having said that, the standard clutch is designed for road use with good and bad drivers in mind, and with a view to it lasting over a very high mileage before needing replacement. It isn't designed to withstand the sustained abuse that an enthusiastic driver of a highly-tuned engine might subject it to.

For those owners wishing to tune their engine to a high level, or compete in their MINIs, there are a number of clutch upgrades available. It's important to upgrade the One/Cooper clutch driven plate when higher tuning or competition is intended as the standard plate will quickly destroy itself under these conditions.

Before embarking upon a clutch upgrade on a road-use only MINI, it's worth bearing in mind that competition grade clutches aren't as user friendly as standard ones. The greater the upgrade the more the clutch will be either 'in' or 'out', there's less slipping available in between, and this means that smooth driving becomes much harder. Many of the upgrades are paddle clutches; paddle clutches are prone to judder, particularly in front-wheel-drive applications. The AP Racing Cooper clutch is a four-paddle plate, it's a driven plate only; they don't produce an upgraded pressure plate, as it wasn't deemed necessary for the application. However, many MINIs are now being tuned to far higher levels than the Cooper S Works spec that is required for the JCW Challenge, so upgrading of the clutch components will be essential in many cases.

At what level is an upgrade required? A good guide can be found in the section on stage tuning earlier in the book. The higher level tuning packages that have been developed by the specialists, in this case notably MED, include a clutch upgrade where it has been deemed necessary.

Paddle style clutch plates are available from Mini Speed for the MINI One and MINI Cooper (they also supply a complete uprated clutch kit for the MINI One & Cooper which includes a pressure plate). Uprated clutch plates are also available for the MINI Cooper S; as is a paddle style plate when further upgrading is required. Additionally there's a full uprated clutch kit for the Cooper S, consisting of a clutch plate, clutch cover/pressure plate and a new release bearing. A new release bearing should always be fitted when the clutch is renewed whether or not the clutch is being upgraded. Good clutch upgrades are also available from Mini Mania.

The standard hydraulic clutch operating system is suitable for all levels of tune and needs no modification.

An uprated
clutch driven
plate with
aligning tool
from Mini
Mania.

Complete clutch
upgrade
package
comprising a
clutch cover,
clutch plate and
release bearing.

the flywheel

The standard flywheel fitted to the MINI Cooper S and One D is of dual mass design. The majority of cars, including the MINI One and Cooper are fitted with a single disc flywheel. A dual mass flywheel differs in that it's made of two discs with a spring mechanism fitted in between. This spring mechanism allows the two parts of the flywheel to rotate independently by up to 70°, and in doing so helps smooth the clutch take up process. Dual mass flywheels also have the advantage of damping down vibration and noise between the engine and transmission, and because of this they're commonly fitted to diesel-engined cars. The vibration insulation is particularly effective when the car's engine is idling.

The dual mass flywheel may be excellent at improving smoothness and in-car comfort but, although it's quite capable of transmitting high levels of power, it isn't the best for maximum performance. Standard flywheels, particularly dual mass flywheels, are also heavy. This is a deliberate design feature on a road car as it helps with the smooth take up of drive and reduces vibration – again, particularly when the engine is idling. The system works well on the standard MINIs which are all very easy to drive smoothly.

From a performance point of view, a single disc lighter weight flywheel is the answer, and a number of suitable flywheels are available for the MINI Cooper S. The standard S flywheel

weighs 12.6kg, while aftermarket replacements can weigh in at under half this amount. It's important to remember that fitting a lightweight flywheel won't increase the power output of the engine. What does happen is that the engine revs will increase more quickly as the throttle is depressed, as the engine has less weight to turn. Acceleration times and responsiveness of the engine will both be improved as a result, and there will be a perceived increase in power from the driver's point of view; also, because of the faster fall and rise of engine revs, the engine will generally feel a lot racier. Therefore, fitting a lightened flywheel is a very worthwhile modification at higher levels of engine tune, and essential for many types of competition. The downside of a lighter flywheel on a road car is that there will be a rougher engine idle, and both noise and vibration levels in the passenger compartment will be increased.

Most tuners offer two weights of flywheel, one for road use and an ultra lightweight flywheel for competition use. Examples of these are Mini Speed's aluminium flywheel; the road version weighs 5kg and the ultra light competition version 4.2kg. The alloy flywheels have a steel friction surface. Another example is the Ultrik flywheel (available from Mini Mania) made of 6061 T6 tempered alloy with a 0.15in thick replaceable steel friction plate. The Mini Mania flywheel is intended for road or mild race use. Lightweight flywheels can be used with both standard and uprated clutch driven plates.

the gearbox

Four different types/versions of manual gearbox have been fitted to the various models in the MINI range. The original MINI One/Cooper gearbox was a modified version of an MG Rover 'box manufactured by Midland Gears, a BMW-owned company.

From July 2004, along with the introduction of the MINI Convertible range, all MINI One and MINI Cooper models were fitted with a new five-speed Getrag gearbox (with modified gear ratios) to replace the Rover-derived unit. The new gearbox provided slightly improved

MINI Cooper S lightened flywheel from MED.

New MINI
gearbox.

torque and bhp figures, and the modification resulted in improved acceleration for both models.

MINI Cooper S models have always been fitted with a six-speed Getrag gearbox, the sixth gear ratio providing a cruising gear, effectively an overdrive to reduce fuel consumption on long journeys. Top speed in the Cooper S is achieved in fifth gear.

The MINI One Diesel is fitted with the six-speed Getrag gearbox from the MINI Cooper S, and has been from introduction, although modified gear ratios to suit the diesel's flatter torque curve are fitted. First gear is a lower ratio, and the other five gears are higher ratio, with sixth gear again effectively being an overdrive for economical and relaxed cruising.

Gearbox modification

The five-speed manual gearboxes fitted to the MINI range are adequate for the standard car and mild levels of tune; they're capable of handling a reasonable level of power increase. However, the Rover-derived gearbox fitted to the One and Cooper up to July 2004 won't cope with huge power increases, and for this reason it isn't the best gearbox if very fast road work or any competition use is intended. The later five-speed Getrag box is a lot stronger.

The six-speed Getrag gearbox on the Mini Cooper S is also much stronger and isn't known for causing problems when the engine is tuned for high outputs. Nevertheless, for very high levels of tune and arduous competition work, modification of even the S gearbox will become both desirable and necessary. A number of very good upgrades are available to improve ratios and increase strength and reliability in both types of 'box. These upgrades come in the form of close-ratio straight-cut gears. Close-ratio gears are just that, the ratios are closer together than in the standard gearbox to minimise the speed loss that occurs with wider spaced ratios. With a close-ratio box the engine can more easily be kept up in the power/torque band to provide swift acceleration out of bends and corners in particular. It's worth noting that when close-ratio gears are fitted the top speed of the car will often be lower than that of the standard

car. However, acceleration and performance throughout the power band will be very much improved. It's this that always wins races, be they on the track or at the traffic lights, rather than out-and-out top speed.

Straight-cut gears have straight-cut teeth rather than the angled teeth found on the standard fitment helical-cut gears. Straight-cut gears are stronger and are capable of transmitting more power, with less power loss, between engine and wheels than helical gears; they also engage faster. Because of this, straight-cut gears are desirable with all high-output engines and in most types of competition where regulations allow. The downside of straight-cut gears when fitted to a road car is increased noise, they also require higher engine revs during driving. These factors should be taken into consideration before fitting to an everyday commuting/shopping MINI.

When a MINI is used in racing, or any type of competition, the gearbox should be rebuilt annually.

Quaife MINI Cooper gear kit

Quaife have recently introduced a five-speed synchromesh gear kit for the MINI Cooper and MINI One. It's suitable for the R63 Rover-sourced early gearbox fitted to MINIs up to 2004. The gears are much stronger than the original items and are helical-cut for quiet operation. Two types are available, close-ratio or Group N. There's an option of a bolt-on crown wheel and pinion, and the original output shaft is retained. The Quaife ATB differential (described in the next section) can be used with this gearbox, but only when the Quaife 3.937 final drive is also fitted.

Quaife Synchromesh gear kit ratios				
1st	2nd	3rd	4th	5th
2.538	1.765	1.421	1.190	1.043

Ultrik five-speed straight-cut close-ratio gear kit

An alternative to the Quaife gear kit is the Ultrik straight-cut close-ratio gear kit for the MINI One and Cooper, which is available from Mini Mania both in the UK and USA. This is a

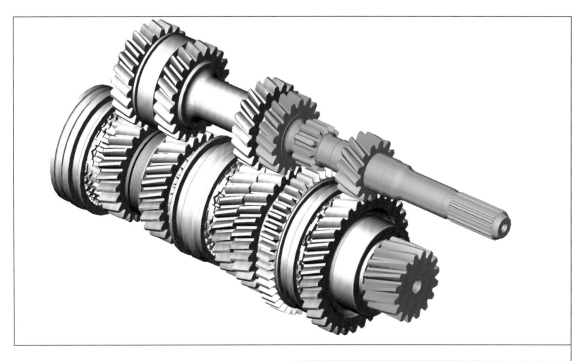

Quaife five-
speed MINI
Cooper gear kit.

dog-engagement style gear set which is
designed to be both very quick-shifting
and durable.

Ultrik SC/CR gear kit ratios				
1st	2nd	3rd	4th	5th
3.417	2.333	1.788	1.429	1.208

Quaife MINI Cooper S dog-engagement gear kit

The Quaife six-speed dog-engagement gear kit is
designed to fit into the standard Cooper S Getrag
gearbox. The kit uses semi-helical close-ratio
gears, and two ratio options are available for fast
road and race use. Final drive ratios are included
in the kit. The Quaife ATB differential is an
optional extra with the dog-engagement gear kit.

Quaife dog-engagement kit ratios					
	1st	2nd	3rd	4th	5th	6th
road	3.846	2.588	1.250	1.029	1.250	1.029
race	3.846	2.737	1.367	1.100	1.367	1.100

Note: This is a two-shaft gearbox, the ratios in
the above table for 3rd and 5th and also 4th
and 6th gears are the same. The two shafts
have separate final drives, which results in
different on-the-road ratios.

Quaife six-speed
dog-
engagement
MINI Cooper S
gear kit.

Ultrik Cooper S close-ratio gears

A close-ratio Ultrik gear kit for the Cooper S is available from Mini Mania. It provides a higher ratio first gear, an appropriately spaced second gear, and a pair of lower final drive ratio gears; a 'pair' of final drive gears is required to make a single change in the 'box. Fitting this gear set will mean that the reverse gear will need to be replaced; the new reverse gear is included in the kit. The reverse gear shift fork will require modification when fitting this gear set.

Ultrik six-speed close-ratio gear set ratios					
1st	2nd	3rd	4th	5th	6th
9.370	7.792	6.516	5.323	4.344	3.549

Standard Cooper S ratios – for comparison					
11.418	7.176	5.399	4.410	3.652	2.984

The gear change

The standard gear change in all manual transmission MINIs is generally smooth and precise, and quick gear changes are easy. The gear lever is connected to the gearbox by means of Bowden cables. For those who wish to upgrade, a quickshift conversion kit to reduce distance between the gear positions is available. Fitting a quickshift shortens the throw of the gear change and gives it a more race-like feel. There are two types of kit depending upon the model year of

the MINI, and more than one manufacturer of both types of kit.

The Ultrik short-shift kit, which is produced by Mini Mania, reduces the gear lever movement between gears by almost 20%. The Ultrik Short Shifter is easier to install than some other one-piece designs as it retains the existing gear lever. An extension is simply slipped on and pinned to the bottom of the standard gear lever. There's no need to remove the gear lever or replace the gear lever knob. All visible components inside the car, including the lever, gaiter and gear knob, remain standard. The Ultrik kit also includes a new bottom dust cover and sealant to protect the modified lever box area. The Ultrik kit fits all MINIs with manual transmission. Two Ultrik kits are available, one for MINIs made up until September 2003 and another for 2004 model year onwards MINIs.

Alternatives to the Ultrik kit come in the form of the Alta quickshift gear lever assembly, which is complete with gear knob. The Alta kit is made of hardened 1144 steel with a black oxide coating to ensure long-term reliability and performance. Steel will also prevent shift-rod distortion from racing style shifts. The kit is fully adjustable to ensure perfect operation.

A further kit is made by B&M; this is similar but doesn't include a gear knob. Both Alta and B&M produce kits for pre- and post-04 MINIs.

Quickshift conversion kit from Mini Mania.

Uprated gear knob

Performance driving is made better with an improved feel gear knob, this is particularly the case when a short-shift gear change has been fitted. Some of the short-shift kits come complete with a gear knob; others will require a knob to be purchased separately. There are a number of different knobs available from manufacturers such as Momo and Richbrook.

Automatic transmission

The MINI One, MINI Cooper and MINI Cooper S are all available with automatic transmission in the form of Continuously Variable Transmission (CVT) with Steptronic. CVT provides normal automatic transmission for driving in traffic and a Sports mode with a six-gear semi-automatic Steptronic transmission. CVT differs from conventional automatic transmission systems in that it's stepless. Conventional systems use a torque converter; but CVT uses an oil bath multi-disc coupling that is electronically controlled. The transmission itself uses a fixed length steel drive belt to connect two double cone-shaped belt pulleys, which transmit the drive from the engine, and this provides infinitely variable transmission ratios. The electronic control comes from the Powertrain Controller, which continuously monitors and adjusts when necessary the position of the cone-shaped pulleys and ensures that the transmission ratio is exactly right for the driving conditions at the time. The adjustment in position is both smooth and constant; hence there are no steps in the system. Sports mode is engaged by moving the gear lever from D to S, and is simply a racier version of the continuously variable operation. The transmission automatically changes from Sports Mode to Steptronic Mode when the driver 'changes gear' manually, which is done by moving the gear lever forwards or back to change up or down in ratio. The shift status is displayed on an LED display, which is located within the speedometer.

In Steptronic mode the main difference from D or S mode is that six electronically-fixed ratios are selected, the transmission is limited electronically in Steptronic to six predetermined ratios. In Steptronic mode the engine can rev higher, up to 6,000rpm. There's a failsafe switching system to prevent errors which could cause damage to the engine or the transmission. Progress from standstill is very smooth with CVT transmission. The electronically-controlled coupling doesn't transmit full power until an engine speed of 2,000rpm has been reached; power produced is restricted and transmitted evenly.

Steptronic paddles for the steering wheel can be specified at additional cost with automatic transmission. Auto-transmission MINIs, especially the Cooper S, are somewhat rare and are probably not as likely to be tuned as manual MINIs. However, the design of the CVT transmission makes it theoretically an excellent box for fast road and competition purposes. Whether or not it's strong enough for very high levels of tune, or robust enough for hard competition use, is as yet unknown because it hasn't been tested. Automatic MINIs can, however, be tuned for the road quite successfully in the same way as manual versions.

the differential and drive shafts

The differential is the set of gears which transmits power from the gearbox through the driveshafts to the wheels. Its purpose is to allow the outer driven wheel to turn faster than the inner wheel when the car is going around a corner or bend. Without a diff, the inner wheel would spin when cornering, and the steering would be heavy and difficult to manage.

All models can be tuned to a significant degree before any upgrading of the standard final drive is needed, but very high levels of tune and competition use will necessitate the need to upgrade. Competition use considerably increases the wear rate on the diff and the diff pin; indeed, rallying and other sports where the car is driven on loose surfaces will wear a standard diff at an unacceptably high rate.

Upgrading the differential

The way to upgrade is to fit a limited-slip differential (LSD). An LSD is designed to prevent

MINI Cooper S
driveshafts.

the complete loss of drive which occurs when one wheel spins with a conventional diff. Three types of differential are available: the Phantom grip from Mini Mania, the Quaife ATB, and the Ultrik LSD. If competition use is intended, the regulations should be checked first, as LSDs aren't permitted in all competitive series and events.

Phantom Grip

The Phantom Grip is the cheapest way to convert the differential to limited slip. The device functions in two ways. First, it serves as a disc-type LSD in cornering and braking (disc plates press against the spider gears using spring pressure to control the amount of slip at the wheels) which helps to maintain grip under acceleration, particularly when coming out of a bend or corner. Second, the Phantom Grip functions as a diff locker under hard acceleration (the disc plates lock the spider gears causing both wheels to receive equal power). The Phantom Grip has been tested over 120,000 miles without showing significant wear, and it comes with a lifetime warranty covering breakage and manufacturing defects.

Another good low-priced diff upgrade is the Mini Gripper limited-slip diff for five-speed 'box available from Mini Speed. This is suitable for the five-speed gearboxes fitted to the One and Cooper.

Quaife ATB

The Quaife ATB differential is available for a number of vehicles. ATB stands for Automatic

Torque Biasing. The unit incorporates a set of floating planetary gears that transmit varying amounts of torque to the wheel that is gripping, depending upon the difference in wheel spin between the two wheels. The whole effect of this is very smooth and progressive, and the differential never completely locks, the result being controlled power transmitted to the driving wheels. This makes the Quaife ATB diff ideally suited to a high-powered front-wheel-drive system such as that in a highly-tuned Cooper S. It also makes the Quaife ATB very suitable for use on the road. The great advantage of this diff is that it doesn't increase torque steer, and therefore doesn't interfere with the steering. The only slight disadvantage is that the ATB diff is heavier than other types of uprated diff. However, this is a minor point which is considerably outweighed by its many advantages.

Installation of the Quaife ATB diff is identical to that of the standard diff, with bearing pre-loads restored to the original manufacturer's settings. Servicing is also straightforward, as all gear pinions are free fitting, and the normal lubricating oil is retained. Because of the internal design of the unit, both driving wheels must be elevated when servicing and repair work is carried out on the brakes or wheels.

The Quaife ATB can be fitted to both the Cooper S with the Getrag gearbox and the MINI One and Cooper with the Rover-derived gearbox, although in the case of the latter a Quaife crown wheel and pinion must be fitted at the same time.

MINI Cooper
driveshafts.

Ultrik Cooper S LSD

The alternative to the Quaife is the Salisbury type limited-slip diff from Ultrik. This LSD is for the Cooper S six-speed transmission, and it can be used on the road as well as for competition. However, the Quaife is the more suitable of the two types for road use, and also has a price advantage. The Salisbury diff is a lighter weight unit, which can cope with 300bhp or more. This is a clutch-type LSD; when one wheel starts to spin faster than the other, hydraulic action moves the clutches within the diff against the spider gears, which transmits power to the wheel which has traction. When this diff is fitted, it's recommended that the front wheel alignment is set up with a minimum of 0.050in toe-in.

Driveshafts

Drive is transmitted to the front wheels by equal length driveshafts – the equal length being achieved by a driveshaft bearing fitted to the engine block. Equal length driveshafts help to eliminate torque steer, which is a common problem in front-wheel-drive cars, particularly those with high power outputs. The standard driveshafts fitted to the MINI are suitable for reasonably high levels of tune, especially if the car is only being used on the road. The Cooper S is fitted with much stronger shafts than the One and Cooper. Cooper S shafts don't normally give trouble, but the One/Cooper shafts will definitely be problematic under competition

conditions. They're simply not up to the job. No upgrades are currently available for either type of shaft, and it's simply a case of monitoring the condition of the shafts if the car is highly tuned.

The Quaife ATB
differential.

The Mini and excellent roadholding have always been synonymous. Great handling was, and remains one of the major appeals of the original car. It was, therefore, absolutely essential that the new MINI should continue the tradition, and it was one of the main design briefs during the initial development of the car. The good news is that even in its standard form the MINI certainly doesn't disappoint. The MINI's centre of gravity is very low and weight distribution is 63% front 37% rear. Add to this the long wheelbase in relation to the overall length of the car, together with the wide track, and it's easy to see why the car handles so well.

the suspension

The suspension set-up consists of MacPherson struts at the front, and a rear axle design that is based on BMW's patented multi-link Z axle. The Z axle is probably best known for its use on the BMW E36 3 Series, a car also known for its excellent road manners. The Z axle design works by allowing the rear road wheels to adjust to the best possible angle in relation to the road in order to maximise tyre contact under all conditions. The original 3 Series design was modified to save space in the smaller MINI and help minimise intrusion into the boot space/passenger compartment. The modified design also helps keep the load floor as low as possible in the rear of the car. The use of the Z axle design was revolutionary in that it was only the second time that it had been fitted to a front-wheel-drive car, and the first time in a small car. It was first used in this configuration in the much larger Rover 75.

All MINIs share the same suspension layout and design; the only variations between the lower- and higher-powered versions of the car are in slightly varying ride height and spring/damper stiffness. The MINI Cooper has uprated Sports Suspension and sits 8mm lower than the MINI One, the MINI Cooper S features the further uprated Sports Suspension Plus package. All models are fitted with a front anti-roll bar, a reinforced bar being fitted to the Cooper and Cooper S, both of which also have a rear anti-roll bar. Traction control (BMW's ASC&T system) is fitted to the Cooper S models as standard; it's optional on the MINI One and Cooper. An upgraded traction system is also available and both systems are described in the following sections.

ASC&T

The ASC&T traction control system is designed to prevent front wheel spin. It uses the ABS sensors on the braking system to detect any wheel slippage, and automatically cuts power to the spinning wheel until grip is restored. The system can be deactivated by the driver who wishes to take the car to its limits, for instance when participating in a track-day event. ASC&T is fitted as standard on the MINI Cooper S and MINI One D, and is an option on the MINI One and MINI Cooper.

DSC

Dynamic Stability Control (DSC) is also available as an option. This is a more sophisticated control system that prevents the car from oversteering or understeering. It increases the vehicle safety level to an even higher standard both through automatic brake applications to individual wheels and the momentary cutting of power to the engine. The DSC option includes ASC&T when specified on models not fitted with ASC&T as standard.

DSC monitors the ABS speed sensors on the wheels, the brake pressure (whether, and how firm, the driver is applying the brakes), the steering wheel lock (to determine the direction in which the car is travelling) and lateral acceleration acting on the car. It therefore considers both the driver's intentions and the current motion of the car, sensing whether the vehicle is deviating

Lowered suspension makes a MINI look a lot more purposeful.

critically from the expected direction of travel. Individual brake applications and changes in the engine torque then correct any deviation.

DSC counteracts oversteer by applying the brake, or increasing the brake pressure if the driver is already braking, on the outer front wheel. This reduces pressure on the wheels facing the inside of the bend, allowing them to grip and pull the car through the bend. To counteract understeer, the DSC control unit applies the brake on the inner rear wheel, taking brake pressure off the outer wheels, and pulling the car back into the bend. When DSC was specified on pre-July 2004 MINI Ones, a rev counter had to be ordered at the same time.

Modifying MINI suspension

There are actually two good reasons for modifying MINI suspension, first and foremost to improve the handling at high speeds and fast cornering, and second for cosmetic reasons; for lowering the suspension won't only improve cornering ability but will also make the car look a great deal more aggressive and sporty. With the correct wheel and tyre

combination, lowering is one of the best appearance mods you can make!

The overall standard MINI handling/ride comfort compromise is impressive and makes all models fun to drive. The ride is also comfortable for a car of its class. The MINI One with standard suspension has a greater degree of ride comfort than the upgraded packages available from the factory. However, when driven very fast all of the models, including the more stiffly sprung Cooper S, tend to feel light at the front end, and for serious performance, especially when the engine has been tuned to a significant degree, upgrading of the suspension system is essential. Lowering by fitting stiffer, shorter springs, and stiffening by fitting upgraded dampers/struts, will improve the handling. There are also a number of other components and upgrade parts available depending upon how far the suspension is to be, or needs to be, improved and also the use to which the car is being put. There are various complete packages available, too. Many are similar, but some are more suitable for certain types of upgrading than others.

Before considering any suspension mods, consider what type of modification is to be carried out to the vehicle. If it's being built as a luxury car with sumptuous upholstery and lots of ICE, softer suspension to improve comfort may be more appropriate than race-tuned lowered suspension.

The factory suspension upgrades
Factory suspension upgrades were standard on higher performance MINIs and were optional on all other models. The factory upgrade parts can also be fitted to models not so equipped, if desired, as an alternative to aftermarket components. This will appeal to anyone tuning their car only to a mild degree or wishing to use original parts only.

Sports Suspension
Sports Suspension is fitted as standard to the MINI Cooper. The same suspension package was available as an option, which could be specified on the MINI One and One D. It does make a significant difference to the way that the car handles at the expense of a slightly stiffer ride. Sports Suspension consists of 8mm lower springs, the anti-roll bar at the front end of the car is stiffened and there's also an anti-roll bar fitted at the rear. The slightly lower ride height does improve the appearance and makes the car look a lot sportier. Many owners originally specified Sports Suspension for this reason alone.

Sports Suspension Plus
Sports Suspension Plus is simply a further uprated version of the Sports Suspension package fitted as standard on the MINI Cooper and optional on the One models. It came as standard equipment on the MINI Cooper S. There are stiffer springs with reinforced anti-roll bars on both front and rear axles to further improve handling and reduce body roll during hard cornering. Sports Suspension Plus was only available as an option on MINI Cooper models, not the One and One D.

Upgrading springs and dampers
Fitting upgraded springs and dampers will have the greatest effect in improving MINI handling. The original suspension is tuned to provide an acceptable level of ride comfort for driver and passengers. Fitting upgraded components will improve the handling, but it will be at the expense of some ride comfort. The stiffer and lower you go, the greater the reduction in ride comfort will be, and this is worth bearing in mind when selecting components. Upgraded springs are the first component to fit. Most of the springs currently available can be used with the standard factory-fitted dampers, although fitting both springs and dampers together will result in a much better overall improvement. If the components are being fitted by a specialist it's advisable to fit both at the same time, as labour costs will be cheaper than trying to spread the costs by fitting springs first and fitting dampers at a later date. Remember though, if the components are being fitted individually, the springs should be upgraded before the dampers.

Lowered springs
Lowering a MINI by fitting shorter springs will make it look a lot better as well as making it corner better. They will lower the centre of gravity of the car, allowing faster cornering

Lowered upgraded front spring from MED.

with reduced body roll. However, it's important to only lower the car by an amount that won't cause difficulty if the car is used on the road. The MINI in standard form is already quite low, roadgoing MINIs can be lowered from 10mm down to about 30mm maximum, but expect some clearance problems over speed bumps, etc. if the car is lowered by the maximum amount. Even the minimum 10mm drop, which is the amount that the car will be lowered using the John Cooper kit, will make a MINI look really good and it will still remain practical on the road. Race cars are normally lowered by 50mm when used only on smooth tracks.

If the suspension is lowered, ideally it should be stiffened at the same time to compensate for the reduced amount of suspension travel and to improve the handling. If lowered springs of the same rate as the originals are fitted, the suspension travel is reduced and there's a real danger that the suspension will continually bottom out over bumps, and this will eventually damage components or the suspension mounting points. The car's occupants will suffer too! When stiffer springs are fitted there will be less shock absorption over bumps, but there will be less body roll on corners and less nose up attitude under hard acceleration, or nose down under heavy braking.

There are several uprated spring sets available, some in varying strengths for different applications. Most general uprated springs are suitable for both road and track-day use. If the car is being prepared for rallying or racing, different parts may be required depending upon the regulations of the events or championship in question. An example of a lowered spring set is that produced by Apex. It's suitable for the MINI One and Cooper and available from Mini Speed. It's available in two versions, one for MINIs manufactured up to March 2002, and the other from April 2002 onwards up until the introduction of the 'Mark 2' new MINI. Both sets of springs will improve handling and reduce body roll. They also lower the standard suspension by 30mm.

Dampers

Dampers, or shock absorbers as they're commonly known, may appear to be just

Far left: Lowered rear spring from MED.

Left: Extreme lowering as on this John Cooper Challenge race car looks fantastic but isn't practical for the road.

simple tubes that bolt to the car and stiffen the suspension. But there's a lot more to them than meets the eye, and the demands on them are very varied. Perhaps the first point to make is that the name 'shock absorber' is technically incorrect for the function that they actually perform. The true shock absorber on a car is the spring, for it's the spring which compresses when the wheel hits a bump, and in doing so, it prevents the full force of the bump being transmitted to the occupants of the car by absorbing some or all of the shock. What is commonly referred to as a 'shock absorber' is in fact a damper, because it damps down the movement of the spring. In doing so it prevents bouncing, which occurs as a form of aftershock following the initial deflection of the spring. It could, of course, be said that in this sense the damper does absorb the shock from the spring, effectively making it a shock absorber to the shock absorber! But 'shock absorbers' are referred to as dampers in this book.

Dampers have to be effective under a variety

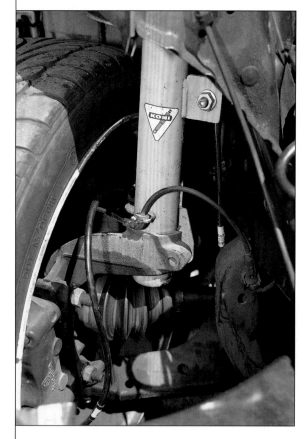

Koni dampers are known for excellent roadholding with comfortable ride.

of conditions. They have to respond in different ways according to conditions, and what is being asked of them at the time. There are basically two types of damping, low speed damping and high speed damping. This isn't a reference to the speed of the car, but the way in which the damper unit responds. Low speed damping is when the damper moves slowly, such as in cornering, where fast movement would cause excessive and immediate body roll. The damper must slowly compress, in other words it needs to be stiff. High speed damping on the other hand needs the opposite reaction from the damper. This is when the wheel hits a bump, perhaps a kerb, or large bumps, as in rallying, and the damper must move quickly to absorb the shock. High speed damping is also required when driving on a motorway; hundreds of quick absorbing reactions are needed to smooth out all the minor imperfections in the road surface. For high speed damping the damper needs to be soft. The only truly perfect way to achieve both high speed damping and low speed damping is with a computer-controlled active suspension system. Although it's possible to build conventional dampers, which are capable of optimum performance under virtually all conditions, the cost is prohibitive. Consequently, as much as anything for reasons of economy, most dampers are a compromise, although an effective one.

The dampers have to be correct for the suspension system of the car to which they are fitted. A car which is under-damped will tend to bounce, and this often happens when the dampers are badly worn. A car which is over-damped will be slow to rise when the suspension is pushed down. A car which is critically damped will have fantastic handling, but unfortunately the driver and passengers will vomit on a regular basis. Formula 1 cars are close to being critically damped. Generally, if the number 1 represents critical damping, the optimum to aim for as far as handling is concerned is around 0.9. Most road cars are in the region of 0.7 to 0.8. Where MacPherson struts are fitted, as they are to the front of the MINI, the strut is much more than just a damper. It's a spring-holder, and a part of the complete suspension system, which also turns with the steering.

Bump, rebound, and adjustment

There are two valves in a twin-tube damper (the type fitted to the MINI), one for bump and one for rebound. Only the rebound action of the damper is actually adjustable, but adjusting the rebound also adjusts the bump stiffness of the damper. The basic principles apply to both the dampers within the MacPherson strut and the rear dampers on a MINI. To understand how and why, it's first necessary to explain the two functions.

Bump

During 'bump' the car's road spring is compressed, and the damper becomes shorter. Inside, a piston, which is attached by a rod to the upper section of the damper, moves within the pressure tube, which is the larger of the two internal tubes. In 'bump' the piston is forced deeper into the pressure tube. The whole of the lower body section of the damper, both above and below the piston, is filled with oil at atmospheric pressure. In the piston are a number of holes, which allow oil to flow from beneath the piston through to the area or 'chamber' above. In this way the oil movement is restricted, and by doing this the damper creates resistance to the motion of the car's road spring. The damping rate (not the adjustment in an adjustable unit) can be varied by introducing obstacles to slow the rate of the flow of the oil. This is done by fitting spring plates over the holes in the piston. Making these spring plates stiffer increases resistance, and stiffens bump damping.

Rebound

Rebound is when the damper is extending. Dampers work on a one-way system, so that in rebound, the bump valve on the piston shuts off and prevents oil passing through the holes. For the damper to extend, oil must return to the lower 'chamber' beneath the piston. With the extending movement, oil is forced out of the top of the upper 'chamber', and flows down the capillary tube. The oil flows through the adjuster valve (in the case of an adjustable damper) at the base of the damper, and back up into the lower chamber beneath the piston in the pressure tube.

Bump to rebound ratio

The bump to rebound ratio is very important. On a typical road car the ratio will be Bump/Rebound 1:3 through to 1:5. On a race car it will be 1:1. A car which is too high on bump will temporarily gradually lower itself if it hits several bumps in succession, whereas if the rebound force is too high, the car will temporarily rise. Damping force requirements are linked to the spring rate of the suspension, the stiffer the spring, the higher the rebound force needs to be.

The adjustment mechanism

The adjustment of dampers with an adjustment mechanism is carried out by means of the valve previously mentioned under 'Rebound'. It's a one-way valve similar in design to the valve in the piston, but designed in this case for maximum flow. The valve is spring-loaded, and returning rebound oil pressure acts against the spring and opens the valve. When the adjuster mechanism is turned to stiffen the damper, the valve spring is compressed, and this increases the force needed to open the valve. This slows the movement of the oil, and in doing so stiffens the damper.

Adjustment is only carried out on the rebound function, but it also stiffens the damper in 'bump' mode. This is because when oil is forced upwards through the piston in 'bump' mode there's less capacity for oil in the upper chamber above the piston than below because of the space occupied by the piston rod. The excess oil is forced out of the top and down the capillary tube through the adjuster valve in exactly the same way as in 'rebound'. Again the tighter the adjuster valve spring, the greater the resistance, and therefore the slower the damper movement.

Car suspension and damping systems have to be a compromise between handling and performance. This is true of all cars, but when the suspension is uprated for performance reasons, the bias is towards handling, and therefore ride comfort will be reduced. Adjustable dampers are generally designed to be roughly equivalent to the standard fitment when they're set at their softest setting. In reality, even on this minimum setting, they're

A SPAX spring and damper unit being fitted to a MINI.

SPAX dampers have a very accessible adjustment mechanism.

Right: Height adjustable damper unit.

Far right: Height adjustment is carried out by varying the position of the spring.

slightly stiffer than standard, and this will often be even more noticeable when they're replacing worn standard units.

Once fitted, the new dampers will need to be correctly adjusted. The adjusters on SPAX front strut units are conveniently located at the top of the strut, meaning that adjustment can be carried out from under the bonnet rather than under the car. Actual settings on adjustable dampers are really down to personal choice, and the type of driving and terrain. The most important thing is to beware of making the dampers too stiff. There are a number of upgraded dampers on the market for the MINI, and which ones to fit will be determined by personal preference and use/competition regulations. At the old John Cooper Works the suggestion was that SPAX are good for fast road, Leda for rallying and Koni and Bilstein for racing. This is only a guideline, and isn't a comprehensive list, and any of the above can be used for anything from road through to competition.

Coil-over kits

Coil-over dampers can be used instead of replacing the springs and dampers separately. Coil-overs have a spring fitted over the damper unit and are fitted to the car after the standard spring and damper have been removed. Good coil-over units are manufactured by SPAX and Leda. Coil-overs are suitable for use on the road, particularly the SPAX units which were developed originally for the John Cooper Challenge race series where the original idea was that the MINI could be driven to the circuit, raced and then driven home again. However, with many coil-overs the ride is much harsher

Far left: Powerflex
upgraded
polyurethane
suspension
bushes.

Left: Large bush
fits front
suspension
arm. Not
recommended for
road use.

than when using the conventional set-up, even when that conventional set-up has been modified. In general, replacement springs and dampers are better for road only use. Coil-overs are often better in certain types of competition.

Upgraded suspension bushes

The MINI suspension can be tightened up, and movement among components reduced, by replacing the standard rubber-type suspension bushes with stiffer polyurethane material. These replacement bushes are 25–30% stiffer than the originals and give increased control over the handling at the expense of an increase in harshness and road noise. Polyurethane bushes are available for the steering rack mounts, the anti-roll bars, the front wishbones and the rear trailing arms, the bump stops and the engine mountings. Polyurethane bushes are loved by some and hated by others. Personally, I'm not a fan. However, if you do like them, they're considered by most tuners, in the case of the MINI, to be far better suited to competition use rather than road use. Solid machined metal

bushes are also available for the rear trailing arms in some markets, but these are strictly for smooth circuit racing only.

Front suspension components
Front end link kit

Upgraded anti-roll bar link kits are available. The front end link kit provides tighter, more responsive handling with the standard fitment anti-roll bar. Alta link kits consist of powder-coated aluminium rods and aircraft-quality Teflon-lined spherical-studded rod ends. These combine to form a fully adjustable, direct connection from anti-roll bar to control arm.

Front strut brace

The MINI bodyshell is already stiff in construction, but for very fast road use or competition the fitting of a front strut brace will offer additional rigidity. With a strut brace fitted, the MINI will feel really solid even under the most extreme cornering conditions. A strut brace is particularly effective with lowered stiffened suspension. Installation can be carried

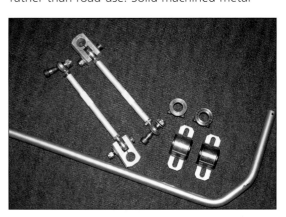

Far left: An
upgraded front
anti-roll bar kit.

Left:
Polyurethane
bushes are also
available for the
anti-roll bar.

Front suspension strut brace will stiffen up the front end. Similar products are available for the rear.

with the road surface, particularly under hard cornering conditions. To describe positive and negative camber very simply: when viewed from the front, if the road wheel leans inwards at the top, the camber is negative; if it leans outwards at the top, the camber is positive. Cornering power is enhanced by negative camber. However, too much negative camber will reduce tyre contact when the car is travelling in a straight line, which is bad for acceleration and will also increase tyre wear on the inside of the tyre.

out easily at home and no setting up is required afterwards. A strut brace is also highly visible when the bonnet is open, and many are fitted for aesthetic reasons only. Strut braces are available from most new MINI tuners, including John Cooper Works accessories.

Caster affects both the feel of the steering and the degree of self-centring of the steering. Caster is best illustrated by looking at a tea trolley; when the trolley is pushed forward the caster angle (i.e. the difference between the centre of the wheel and the pivot of the steering) causes the wheels to self-centre and allows the trolley to move in a straight line. A similar effect can be found on the front forks of a bicycle. In a car the greater the degree of caster the greater the effort needed by the driver to turn the steering wheel. If there's too little caster, the steering will be over light and

Front camber and caster angles

The handling and steering of any car is affected by the camber and caster angles. Camber is the angle of the road wheel, and it determines how much of the tyre tread will be in contact

Adjustable front top strut mount shown here in component form.

will have little or no self-centring action. For high-performance driving, caster can be increased, and for competition use it can be further increased. Camber on roadgoing MINIs is pre-set at 2° to 2½° negative front. For racing the front is normally set at 3° to 3½°.

Adjustable front strut top mount kit

On a MINI, caster and camber are determined by the mounting point of the top of the front MacPherson struts. Adjustable strut tops are available to replace the standard plates, and these allow accurate adjustment of both camber and caster. They're available for both the standard design coil and separate damper assemblies, and also for coil-over damper conversions. Adjustment can be made without jacking the vehicle up, but specialist alignment equipment is required to determine the settings.

Rear suspension components

There are a number of rear suspension improvements that can be made to enhance the MINI's handling.

Camber adjuster plates

Camber at the rear on roadgoing MINIs is pre-set at 1½° negative. For racing, a maximum of 3° at the rear is normally recommended. A snail cam allows 1° of adjustment at the rear on a standard MINI. Further camber adjustment is carried out at the rear by means of an adjustable camber rear bush kit. These are normally supplied with a bush-removing tool to allow easy installation. Setting up is required using specialist equipment.

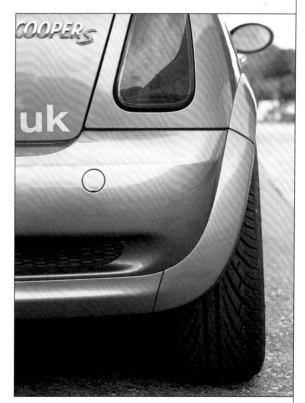

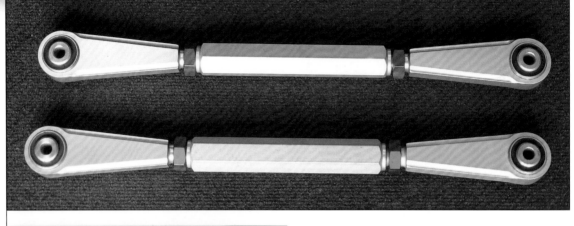

For greater adjustment, adjustable rear control arms must be fitted.

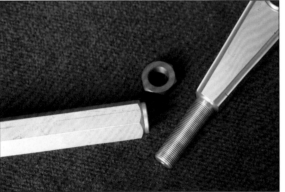

These adjust by a considerable amount.

Upgraded rear control arms

A more serious mod is to fit upgraded rear suspension control arms. Under extreme conditions the standard rear suspension arms can be prone to flexing, and stronger arms will give a more solid feel to the handling of the car. Two types are available: fixed chromoly arms, and alloy adjustable arms. As well as tightening up the rear end, the alloy adjustable type of arm also has the advantage of allowing both camber and wheel alignment to be adjusted.

Alta rear suspension arms are fully rose-jointed and have a continuous hardened-steel tube, direct bored and threaded to accept heim-joint ends. Threaded into both rod ends are aircraft-quality, Teflon-lined, heim-joint rod ends. The Teflon lining prevents road vibration from being transferred through the joint, and constantly cleans the bearing surface. A 22mm flat notch is built into the end of the rod for easy adjustment. These adjustable type arms are more expensive than the rear camber kits

described above, but they offer a greater range of adjustment and are easier to adjust.

Rear anti-roll bar

The MINI Cooper S is fitted as standard with a rear anti-roll bar (or anti-sway bar as they're known in the USA). The purpose of this is to cut down on the amount that the car understeers in fast bends and corners. Understeer is when the front of the car continues to move forward in a straight line when the wheels are turned, and more steering lock has to be applied resulting in the front wheels moving sideways in the corner. Oversteer is when the rear of the car 'hangs out' on a bend. As a general rule, front-wheel-drive cars such as the MINI understeer and rear-wheel-drive cars oversteer. An anti-roll bar is a bar which links the two wheels on one axle. It's connected to the suspension arms close to the wheels by lever arms or links, and the bar itself is fitted to the chassis of the car using rubber bushes and brackets. When one wheel is forced upwards or downwards under cornering, the opposite wheel moves in the other direction, i.e. one wheel goes up the other down, resulting in body roll. An anti-roll bar helps reduce this effect, and in doing so helps keep the car level and reduces body roll. If the rear of the MINI is kept more level there's less pressure on the front wheels, and the car will corner more effectively with reduced understeer.

The standard Cooper S anti-roll bar is 13mm thick and designed to offer a good compromise between fast road handling and ride comfort. The handling of the car can be improved by fitting a thicker bar, which will preferably be adjustable. Such a bar is the Ultrik dual use anti-roll bar which has sliding attachment points at either end, which when moved vary the stiffness of the bar from harder to softer. This is particularly useful if the MINI is to be used for track days. An Alta adjustable rear anti-roll bar, which is 19mm thick, is also available. The Alta bar has two different end link attachment points. Both bars are recommended for road or track use. They can be fitted to the Cooper S to upgrade the standard bar with good results, and they can also be fitted to the MINI One and Cooper. For really serious competition, thicker anti-roll bars can be fitted. An example of this is the Alta adjustable 22mm rear anti-roll bar. Thicker bars can make the car less pleasant to drive on the road under normal driving conditions, and should be matched to correct-strength heavy-duty springs and dampers.

Rear end link kit

As with the front anti-roll bar, rear end anti-roll bar link kits are available. The improvements are similar to those of the front end kits in providing generally tighter, more responsive handling.

Rear strut brace

For very serious competition work, such as autocross, some owners fit a rear strut brace to further stiffen the bodyshell. The rear brace fits to the upper suspension mounts, in the same manner as at the front, and is easily installed. This is a mod for serious competition work only and isn't necessary on a fast road car.

Suspension tuning packages

Most of the suspension manufacturers and MINI specialists offer complete suspension upgrade packages. These kits are complete in their own right in achieving a certain degree of improvement in handling, but complete in this instance doesn't mean that every available upgrade component is included in the package! These kits are generally designed for use on the road, although some will be suitable for the basis of competition suspension depending upon regulations and the type of competition envisaged. Good upgrade units are available from Leda, Spax, Gaz, and Bilstein. Most of these systems are fully adjustable for both height and stiffness and will lower the car by up to 30mm (Gaz), or 40mm (Bilstein). It's important to select the correct kit to best suit driving style and conditions. The Spax kit, for

A John Cooper Works suspension unit on show in the old JCW premises.

The JCW Works kit lowers a road MINI by just the right amount. Handling, too, is much improved.

instance, allows lowering between 15mm and 50mm and is adjustable on the car, making it ideal for track days and road use. Many of the other systems offer similar ranges. Suspension kits are sold by John Cooper Works and Birds (Hartge).

Mini Speed offer several kits. The Suspension Upgrade Kit 1 consists of the Eibach lowered-spring set, and an uprated 19mm rear anti-roll bar. The Suspension Upgrade Kit 2 consists of the Eibach lowered-spring set, uprated 19mm rear anti-roll bar, adjustable rear camber bush kit, and adjustable front strut top mount kit. The Suspension Upgrade Kit 3 includes Eibach lowered-spring set, uprated 19mm rear anti-roll bar, adjustable rear camber bush kit, and adjustable front strut top mount kit, plus rose-jointed front and rear drop links, and front brace. Suspension packages are often a good way to improve the road holding of a roadgoing MINI, as when supplied by a reputable specialist they will have been developed to work to the level intended and there won't be any mismatching of components.

Suspension settings

Different suspension upgrade systems will require different height and stiffness settings. Just how hard and low the suspension is adjusted will depend very much on how and where the car is going to be driven. For both height and damper adjustments it's best to use the manufacturer's or

supplier's recommendations as a starting point; the settings can be tuned for personal preference later.

Correct alignment

Although there are a number of references to correct specialist setting-up of modified suspension, it must be emphasised that whatever is done in the way of suspension modification it's vitally important to have the suspension correctly set up and aligned afterwards. If this isn't done, the handling may well be ruined and the car may be dangerous at high speed, as well as suffering from much increased tyre wear. Suspension and wheel alignment can be carried out by MINI dealers and most suspension specialists.

Steering

The petrol-engined MINI's rack-and-pinion power steering is very responsive and offers excellent feedback through the steering wheel. It requires 2.5 turns from lock to lock. The power system is unusual in that it's 'electrohydraulic' – the hydraulic pump is powered by an electric motor rather than being engine-driven. The pump produces a characteristic whine when the steering wheel is turned, which is unique to the MINI. The MINI One D has an engine-driven power steering pump. No modifications are available or necessary to the system other than fitting a different steering wheel if so desired.

the brakes

All MINI models are equipped with diagonal dual-circuit disc brakes all round. The front discs are 276mm x 22mm and are ventilated, the rears are solid and are 259mm x 10mm. The braking system includes the BMW Group standard electronic brake control and stability systems, four-sensor anti-lock braking system (ABS), electronic braking distribution (EBD) and cornering brake control (CBC).

EBD controls the braking force between the front and rear wheels to ensure correct braking power distribution under different loads and conditions. EBD is activated under average braking pressures, a long time before ABS would normally kick in. Unlike ABS, EBD isn't detectable by the driver and cannot be deactivated by the driver.

CBC prevents the car from becoming unstable when braking through corners. The electronic system detects side slip of the wheels via the ABS sensors if the car becomes unstable. This can occur if the brakes are applied heavily while cornering. The system recognises that the car is cornering, and feeds more braking force to the outside front wheel when necessary, reducing the possibility of sliding or skidding. The brakes on MINIs work well and are more than capable for the standard car under normal road conditions, and indeed also cope well with spirited driving. However, for track-day use, modified fast road cars, and those used in competition, the brakes must be upgraded.

Upgrading the brakes

Upgrading the brakes on a tuned MINI will not only make the car safer, it will effectively make it quicker as the uprated engine performance can be more fully used, and the added security will make the car more fun to drive – a safe well-balanced performance car is an enjoyable car.

MINI brakes can easily be upgraded; first, by fitting improved brake pads; second, by upgrading the discs (this will improve the brakes sufficiently for most road applications); and third by fitting larger calipers. Good quality upgrade pads and discs are made by EBC, and there are a number of other good components

The standard MINI front brakes. For serious performance MINIs the brakes need to be upgraded.

on the market. Many people choose to fit one of the complete upgrade kits that are available.

When fitting larger brakes, in particular larger upgraded calipers, 17in or 18in wheels are often required. With all big brake

All MINI front brakes use vented discs from standard up to fully modified.

First stage upgrade is performance brake pads.

brakes. The hotter the brakes get, the less efficient they become and the driver will have to push much harder on the brake pedal to bring the vehicle to a halt. Eventually, if pushed hard enough, the brakes will overheat so much that they won't work at all. This is known as brake fade and is a problem common to all road cars, but only when being driven to extremes! The problem is easily overcome and, as stated, the first requirement is to fit upgraded disc pads.

Upgraded pads are made of harder material and will require greater effort when cold to stop the car, but will operate more efficiently at hotter temperatures, meaning much more effective braking on a hard-driven performance car. There are a number of different grades of pad available for the MINI, some for fast road use others purely for competition use. If the MINI is to be used on the road it's important not to fit too hard a pad. Pads that are designed for racing are ineffective at low speeds until they have warmed up – something that they won't do under normal road conditions. Good road performance all round upgrade pads are EBC Greenstuff. Fitting these will reduce brake fade considerably without substantially increasing pedal effort or reducing cold braking performance.

conversions it's advisable to check wheel clearance before buying and fitting. Some kits recommend the fitting of wheel spacers to obtain clearance. These are important points to consider when deciding how far you need to go in upgrading brakes.

Brake pads
Fitting upgraded brake pads is the first step in improving MINI braking performance, and it's a straightforward and inexpensive upgrade. The standard road pads are made of relatively soft material to keep the effort required from the driver fairly low. The problem with these under high-speed conditions, when harder and longer braking is required, is that the pads heat up quite quickly, reducing the efficiency of the

Upgraded discs
Heat generated by friction when the brakes are operated causes the brake pads to heat up, and naturally the discs heat up too. Also, under hard use there will be a build-up of dust and pad residue on the discs, and both of these factors will reduce the effectiveness of the

Right: Discs are next to be upgraded.

Far right: Rear discs are upgradable too.

Tarox upgrade kit for one front side from MED.

brakes when driving hard. Fitting higher-performance brake pads will certainly improve matters, but to make high-performance pads really effective, upgraded discs are also needed. There are a number of good upgraded discs on the market. Upgrading is achieved by fitting drilled and slotted discs – drilling the discs helps to dissipate heat, and slotting them (machining grooves across the surface of the disc from the centre to the outer edge) helps with cooling by allowing air to pass between the pad and the disc. The grooves or slots also create a channel through which the dust that builds up on the surface of the pad can escape. Also, the grooves help clean the pads every time the pad passes over them. Cleaner, cooler brakes are more efficient brakes. Upgraded discs for the

MINI are available – vented for the front and non-vented for the rear.

Big brake upgrades

All the upgraded discs described above are of standard dimensions. When very serious modifications have been carried out to the engine, or the car is to be used in racing, the brake upgrading should include larger-diameter brake discs and larger calipers. Larger brakes are much more effective, and the greater surface area of the components means more effective heat dissipation. Larger brake conversions for MINIs come in complete kits, and there are several good kits available.

The most important thing to remember when considering a larger brake conversion is that a minimum wheel diameter of 17in is required with many kits. Some kits will even require 18in wheels. It's vital to check with the manufacturer or supplier that the kit will fit under the particular wheels on your MINI. The diameter of the standard front discs on a MINI is 276mm and the discs are 22mm thick. Big brake conversions use discs which vary in diameter from 300mm through to 328mm, hence the reason for usually requiring larger diameter wheels for clearance. Big disc thickness goes up from 22mm standard to between 23mm and 28mm depending upon

Far left: Close up on Tarox six-pot caliper.

Right: Big brake upgrades enhance the appearance of the running gear. This is a rear upgrade.

Far right: Brembo big front brake kit fitted.

the kit. Larger calipers are always required with larger discs.

Some examples of big brake kits are as follows:

The AP Racing big brake kit. Considered by many to be the ultimate brakes for use with some of the most powerful engine conversions, the AP kit consists of cross-drilled 304mm x 24mm 40-vane diameter discs with red-coloured four-pot calipers, a set of fast road or race pads, a set of braided flexible hoses, and all the necessary fittings and fasteners, plus some DOT 5.1 brake fluid. The calipers have dust seals,

there are anti-rattle clips for the pads, and an anti-corrosion finish making the brakes suitable for everyday road use. This type of durable specification is something to check for on all calipers intended for road use. Some makes of aftermarket alloy calipers, in particular, don't include dust seals, and their life on a road car can be severely shortened by this.

The AP kit will make a massive difference to a MINI's stopping power. As the AP brake calipers are much larger than the standard ones, 21mm wheel spacers are recommended with most wheels. This is a point to check before buying (see above). *John Cooper Works*

JCW big brake kit.

also supply a complete MINI big brake kit of their own which is based on AP Racing components and consists of larger brake discs and brake calipers at the front, with special brake pad linings on the rear.

The Wilwood High Performance Brake kits. The Wilwood big brake kits are a very popular fitment to roadgoing and competition MINIs alike. There's more than one version of the kit to cater for different applications. All of the kits consist of Wilwood Midilite four-pot ally calipers, coloured black, with drop-forged body and fully dust-sealed, complete with 1in and ⅜in pistons. The first kit comes with 310mm x 21mm vented road discs, and polymatrix 'E' grade brake pads. The next kit contains upgraded 310mm x 21mm vented and cross-drilled road discs, together with the polymatrix 'E' grade brake pads. The ultimate kit, intended for competition, is the Wilwood Racing/Rallying big brake kit. This contains the same calipers but features 300mm x 21mm cross-drilled and vented race-spec discs, and polymatrix 'E' grade brake pads.

Brembo produce a big brake kit with floating front discs. These discs are 320mm x 28mm

All sorts of upgrades can be fitted. This MINI is equipped with Porsche brakes.

and are both vented and cross-drilled. Four-piston alloy calipers come with the kit and are available in a variety of colours.

Hartge/Birds. Birds offer a Hartge Sports front brake kit which contains the largest available discs for fitting to a MINI. These are 328mm x 28mm floating front discs, complete with 7075 T-6 billet aluminium mounting bells, a pair of ST 40 four-piston calipers and stainless steel brake lines. You'll need 18in wheels if fitting this kit.

Some of these brake kits include replacement pads for the rear brakes. Harder brake pads

Far left: When upgraded calipers are fitted, the right alloy wheels show them off nicely.

Left: With some alloys, keeping the brakes clean is essential.

must be fitted to the rear brakes when fitting larger brakes to the front, to maintain the balance of the braking system. An additional advantage of brake upgrades involving replacement calipers is that they add to the custom appearance of the car – most upgrade calipers look really good and are painted in bright colours and are highly visible through the spokes of the alloy wheels.

Braided brake hoses

Like most production cars, the MINI is fitted with rubber type flexible brake hoses. When the brakes are applied hard, some expansion of the hoses takes place even when they're new or in good condition. As the hoses become older, or have been subjected to hard use, the problem magnifies. As the brake fluid from the master cylinder enters the flexible hoses before it can reach the brake calipers there's a loss of efficiency if the hose balloons slightly. The way to overcome the problem is to fit a set of stainless steel flexible hoses; these are made of PTFE internally and covered with braided stainless steel. This construction virtually eliminates any expansion and gives a much more solid feel to the brake pedal, especially under heavy braking conditions. Stainless brake hoses are normally fitted to competition cars, but are highly suitable and recommended on high-performance road MINIs as well.

The handbrake

The standard equipment handbrake works well and there's no need to carry out any modification to upgrade it from a performance point of view. The only thing that can be done to the handbrake is to replace the lever with a fly-off one. This was a popular modification to original Minis in the 1960s and early 1970s, and is particularly useful in certain types of competition.

Brake hoses can be upgraded to the braided Goodridge type of hose.

Right: Goodridge hose in situ.

Far right: Fly-off handbrake conversion demonstration unit alongside the standard lever.

wheels and tyres

One of the most important areas when modifying any vehicle is the choice of wheels and tyres. In fact, it's true to say that the choice of wheels and suitable tyres is probably the most significant modification that will be made to a MINI. This is because, first, the overall style of the modified vehicle is greatly influenced by the design, the width, and the diameter of the wheels, and second, the wheel and tyre combination greatly affect the handling and road manners of the car. We have already established elsewhere in this book that all the models in the MINI range handle well as standard, and this applies even to the MINI One and One D in their most basic versions with narrowest available 165/55R15 tyres on steel wheels. The 16in and 17in wheel options with the 195/65R16 tyres provide grippier and more precise handling.

One important point to note when changing wheels is that larger diameter wider alloys need to be fitted to a car with suitable height suspension. Wheels over 16in diameter do need lowered suspension to look good (even 16s do, really). With standard height suspension, large diameter wheels make a car look very tall and will create the impression of a slower car. There's nothing like wider wheels and lowered suspension to make a car look faster and more aggressive.

Factory alloys

There was a very large range of alloy wheels in 15in, 16in and 17in styles available as optional equipment from the factory on new MINIs, and most styles are available from MINI dealers for retro fitment. Fitting genuine MINI alloys as an upgrade does keep the car more original, if this is important, and does ensure that the quality of the wheels chosen is suitable. A number of

Far left top: A 15in alloy fitted to a MINI One D. This size of alloy is a big improvement over the standard steel wheel but still needs to be upgraded on a performance-tuned MINI.

Far left bottom: Cooper S alloys are a big improvement.

Left: S alloys will go a long way to improving a One or Cooper.

Alloy wheel
selection on
display at a MINI
specialist.

different alloy wheel options are available across the MINI range, with a further exclusive design being available for the Convertible models. As the hubs and brakes are the same throughout the range this means that any factory wheel can be fitted on any model.

Factory wheels are often available second-hand, being sold by people who are upgrading to larger diameter and perhaps wider aftermarket wheels. It's very important to ensure that any wheels bought second-hand are in good sound condition. Ideally they should be bought from a known source, and if there's any doubt the wheels must be checked by a specialist for any damage or cracking. Fitting alternative factory wheels might not at first sound very appealing but a set of Cooper S alloys, for instance, will certainly upgrade a set of MINI One steels and completely transform the appearance of the car.

The following is a quick guide to what was fitted to MINIs at the factory:

■ Two 15in alloy designs were available on MINIs as standard, these being the R81 5.5x15 seven-hole on the Mini Cooper, and the R82 eight-spoke. Both wheels take a 175/65R15 tyre, and both are available in silver or white finish.

■ The 16in light alloy wheel option was the 6.5x16 R83 five-star available in silver (or white finish optional on cars with a white roof). This was fitted with a 195/55 R16 tyre.

■ The 17in light alloy wheel optional was the R85 7x17 S-spoke which came in silver or white and requires a 205/45R17 tyre.

Aftermarket alloys

For those wanting a more exclusive look, there are numerous aftermarket alloy wheel designs to choose from. One that is particularly worthy of note is produced by Minilite who supplied the alloys for the original BMC Works rally Minis back in the 1960s and early 1970s. The 7x16in wheel for the new MINI was produced to celebrate Minilite's 40th year in wheel manufacturing, and it will fit all new MINI models. Other exclusive very nice wheels are made by Hartge: these are larger diameter 18in wheels and come in two designs, the Classic and a MINI special Union Jack design. Another stylish alloy wheel is made by Hamann Motorsport, a well-known German company which produces a number of upgrade components for BMW – this is a five-spoke design in silver with a polished outer rim and is available in 17in and 18in diameters.

A very good range of wheels is the Image three-piece split rims. There are several styles and each design is available in a number of sizes. There are many other wheels, too; far too many to detail here. For individual choice it's best to visit one of the larger new MINI specialists.

The right alloys show off brake calipers nicely, as on this Mini Mania prepared MINI.

Wheel picture gallery: There's a huge choice of alloy for all MINI models, both genuine MINI and aftermarket.

Think carefully about your choice of alloy. Nineteen-inch alloys need body modification and can look over-the-top on an otherwise outwardly standard MINI.

Bodywork clearance

The larger the diameter of wheel fitted to the MINI, the greater the chance of fouling the bodywork, even when super-low-profile tyres are fitted. With all the factory sizes there shouldn't be any problems, but whenever fitting larger wheels it's advisable to check clearance carefully. Eighteen-inch wheels are the largest that should be fitted to a MINI, and even then, with many designs, some wheel arch modification will usually be necessary.

Some people have gone even larger in diameter than this and have fitted 19in or 20in wheels. With these there will definitely be wheel arch rubbing problems, and wheel arch modification will be required. Most tuners agree that very large diameter wheels such as 19in and 20in look far too big on a car the size of the MINI, although there are exceptions on some bodykitted highly-modified MINIs. As a general rule, it's best to stick to 16in, 17in or, if you want large, 18in. Not only will your MINI look better, it will also handle better and will ride better, too. From a ride comfort point of view, don't go over 16in diameter wheels.

Wheel and tyre security

A locking wheel nut kit is essential if expensive alloys are fitted. These are available from MINI and from most specialists, and provide increased peace of mind.

Tyres

Once suitable wheels have been selected, or purchased, they will need to be fitted with the correct size tyres. Tyres are very important, not just for road holding but also for looks. Many people make the mistake of buying a nice expensive set of wheels and then try to save money by fitting budget tyres. This is a big mistake. Good quality performance tyres have a big effect upon handling, and they will always look better, too. And they will generally be longer lasting. Budget quality tyres are for budget quality cars. Good tyres are made by Yokohama, the A539 comes in 205/50x16, 205/45x17 and 205/40x17. Birds fit Pirelli P7000 215/35x18 tyres to the 7.5x18 Hartge rims on their cars. These are just two examples, and the best advice is to stick to one of the premium brands and check what is the best current performance tyre with MINI specialists.

Spare wheels and run-flat tyres

Instead of carrying a spare wheel, the MINI is equipped with the MINI Mobility System. This consists of a sealant and a compressor that is stored in the boot. In the event of a puncture the tyre pressure warning indicator will alert the driver, who must then stop and fill the tyre with sealant via the valve. Tyre pressure can then be restored using the compressor. Sixteen-inch run-flat tyres are supplied with the MINI Cooper S; these tyres have reinforced sidewalls and are made from heat-resistant rubber. Functions such as ABS, ASC&T or DSC aren't affected if pressure is lost and the driver can continue the journey for up to 80 miles at speeds of up to 50mph. Even if fully deflated, the tyres can safely run at 30mph.

Run-flat tyres were only available on 16in wheels and were an option on MINI One, MINI One D, and MINI Cooper. An improvement in handling, and certainly an improvement in ride comfort, will come from swapping run-flat tyres to conventional tyres, and this action is definitely best on seriously modified MINIs.

Good tyres will improve handling and appearance.

The MINI Cooper S with John Cooper Works GP Kit features specially designed lightweight 18in alloy wheels.

06 the body and interior

Modifying a car, particularly when it comes to the bodywork, is all about improving its looks, often following a particular theme and resulting in a car which stands out from the crowd. Because of its distinctive and unique looks, the MINI has a head start even before any modification is considered.

the MINI bodyshell

Bodyshell stiffness is very important in a car, both from handling and safety points of view, and MINI body stiffness is two to three times greater than that of the competition. It has one of the stiffest body structures that BMW has produced, its torsional strength being equal to that of the E46 3 Series. Stiffness also affords crash protection. During an impact, energy can be absorbed by the crush zones and directed away from the occupants, whilst the body acts as an effective passenger protection shell.

The MINI certainly scores well from a safety point of view. It was designed to reach the NCAP 4-star crash test rating, and to improve the impact characteristics a lot of work went into engine alignment and engineering of the front axle to absorb energy from the floorpan. Further energy-absorbing zones were designed

in to prevent footwell intrusion. Reassurance of this nature is good in any car, but especially so when the car is modified and maximum performance has been squeezed out of it.

As well as the MINI saloon, the MINI Convertible is popular for all types of modification, including bodywork. Like the saloon, the Convertible is highly distinctive, particularly with the roof down, and the shell is designed in such a way that it doesn't require a B post. BMW say that the structure is so stiff that it will handle in exactly the same way as the saloon versions.

With a Convertible body, safety becomes even more important because of the lack of protection which would normally be given by the steel roof. To compensate for this lack, the MINI Convertible has reinforced side sills. This helps to minimise scuttle shake and also helps prevent deformation of the shell in the event of both frontal and side impacts. An extra strong floorpan, additional

Distinctive in standard form, a few modifications to the bodywork will make a MINI stand out even more.

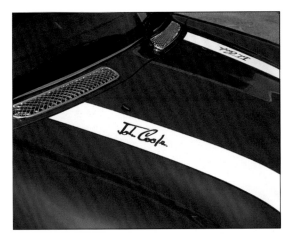

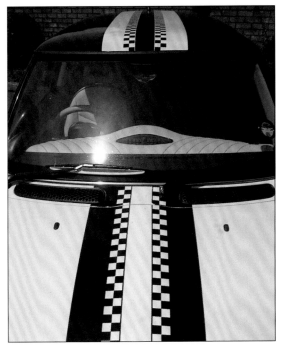

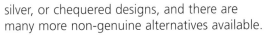

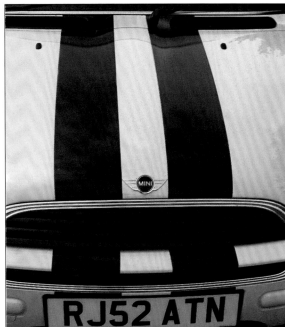

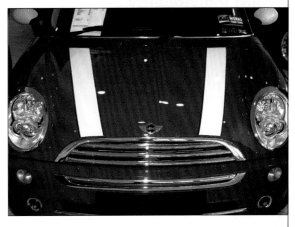

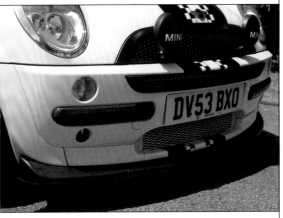

Bumper inserts come in a number of styles.

MINIWagon
front. *(Castagna
Milano)*

MINIWagon
back. *(Castagna
Milano)*

Genuine MINI and JCW upgrades ...

crossbars and thicker body panels have also been designed in at all critical points. The front end of the car is identical in structure to the fixed roof model. To protect the occupants in the event of a roll the A pillars are reinforced with a high strength steel tube, which is capable of absorbing 1½ times the mass of the car. There's also a roll-bar made of high strength aluminium built into and around each of the rear head restraints. This serves as a roadster-like styling feature – almost a mod before you even start.

'Tuning' the bodywork

Before beginning any work on the bodywork it's important to decide upon the style or theme you wish to work to. Body mods are, after all, the most visual of modifications; they will say a lot about you as the owner, and they will either

... subtle distinction and genuine upmarket appearance.

Big wheels and colour-coding on a Cool New prepared MINI One.

make or break the final appearance of the car. There are so many options to choose from, such as privacy glass, wider wheel arch extensions, and the results can be anything from the battered well-used look of a well-hammered street racer through to complete bespoke coachbuilding.

MINI Individuality

It's possible to create a very individual MINI purely by using genuine MINI parts and accessories. There was a huge range of options available when the cars were new, and an equally large range of upgrade parts and accessories for retro fitment. BMW have nearly always been very strong on options, and the basic list price of most of their models is a long way from the average price paid for the cars. That range of options and opportunities to create a very individual MINI continues with the very latest versions of MINI models.

The bespoke nature of MINI production

allows mixing and matching of components and equipment, meaning that it's possible to produce tens of thousands of different MINIs – the cars coming down the production line at any given time are being built to individual specification. Factory options range from different alloys through to bodykits.

There are many more smaller dress-up parts, such as chrome side repeater vents, clear light lenses and additional front driving lamps, and a four-lamp Works spot lamp kit with a stainless steel lamp bar. Described below are some of the more popular personalising mods, some factory, some MINI accessories, some aftermarket.

Bonnet stripes

Bonnet stripes, reminiscent of the 1960s Cooper Works racing Minis, and the 1990s special edition original Mini Coopers, are available and very popular on the MINI. Genuine parts are available in white, black,

Right: A spoiler and stripes create a very different look on this Cooper S.

Far right: A nicely turned out Cooper S Works.

Far left: Bonnet stripes are popular on the MINI and available from MINI and aftermarket.

Left: Bold stripes add vibrance to the car.

RJ52 ATN

Far left: Variation on the black on yellow theme.

Left: Red on white is a classic Cooper scheme.

silver, or chequered designs, and there are many more non-genuine alternatives available.

Bumper inserts

The front and rear bumper inserts on the One and Cooper models are supplied as standard in body colour, but black inserts could be specified at extra cost, although this option wasn't available on the Cooper S. Most people went for the Chrome Line Exterior option, which meant that the front and rear bumper inserts are chrome plated. Other genuine and non-genuine options, such as carbon fibre, are also available.

DV53 BXO

Bumper inserts come in a number of styles.

Tinted windows

Tinted windows are standard across the whole MINI range, as they are on virtually every car made today. It's possible to go a shade further and have a top tinted windscreen, and darker tinted glass on the other windows can also be fitted. If you're going to use film to create privacy glass in the rear side windows it's best to get it applied by a specialist, as it's very difficult to do without creating a lot of air bubbles.

Roof decal options

The Cooper and Cooper S came with a white or black roof as standard, and the door mirrors were coloured to match the roof. The numerous roof decal options make a good way of personalising your car. Most of the decals are available for black, white or body-colour roofs, but there are some exceptions. The available genuine MINI designs include the following: Target (which consists of red, white, and blue circles); Spider web; Stars and stripes (the USA flag); Zebra Print; Lion Rampant; St Andrew's Cross; Welsh Flag; Silver Union Jack (this is available on black-coloured roofs only); St George's Cross; Canadian Flag; Chequered

Flag; Viper Stripes (which are available in black, white, or silver); and the Union Jack. Roof decals can, of course, only be fitted to solid roofs; they aren't available with the sunroof option for obvious reasons. The most popular roof decal in the UK and the USA is the Union Jack.

These are just the official MINI options. A graphics company would be able to produce virtually any design according to individual taste.

Sunroofs

For those not requiring a roof decal there was the option of a factory-fitted, electrically-operated panoramic slide and tilt sunroof. This is a very large sunroof, and it opens up to almost one-and-a-half times the size of a conventional sunroof. It also has a back section of solid glass fixed in position behind the opening section, which does create a very spacious atmosphere inside the car.

If you don't have a factory-sliding sunroof, then it's possible to fit a fabric folding sunroof. Made by Webasto, this highly traditional MINI accessory is electrically powered with one touch operation and two pre-set opening positions.

Roof decals are popular and are available as genuine MINI accessories or from aftermarket manufacturers.

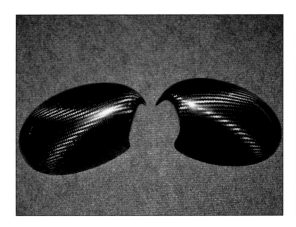

Far left: Mirror covers come in numerous styles from carbon fibre …

Left: … through Union Jack …

Mirror covers

For a different look from the standard door mirror covers that are finished in white or black, there are mirror gloves made of stitched vinyl, giving a touch of the vintage look. There are masses of other options, including chequered and flag designs, both MINI parts and aftermarket.

For MINIs with the Chrome Line Exterior it's possible to continue the theme onto the door mirrors. Although this in theory provides a retro look, MINI door mirrors are quite large and the expanse of chrome won't suit all tastes, so it's not a bad idea to take a look at a car so equipped before ordering.

… chrome and many more.

Fitting an S bonnet scoop to MINI One and Cooper

The main distinguishing difference between the MINI Cooper S and the lesser-powered models is the Cooper S's intercooler bonnet scoop. It's possible to fit the bonnet scoop to the bonnet of the One and Cooper, but a great deal of work is involved, and this work will need to be carried out by a skilled panel beater. If you must have a bonnet scoop, it would certainly be quicker and probably cheaper to fit the Cooper S bonnet. The S bonnet is a straight swap for the Cooper/One bonnet.

S bonnet scoops can be fitted to the Cooper and One, but the easiest way is to fit an S bonnet.

MINI One and Cooper front bumper mesh

The black plastic grille on the MINI One and the alloy grille on the MINI Cooper can be replaced with a laser-cut brightly-polished stainless steel grille which clips onto the existing tabs. This mesh grille won't fit the MINI One D models,

The lower grille mesh can be changed.

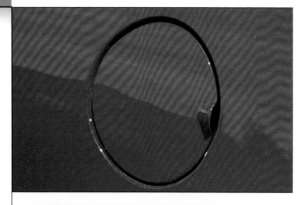

The standard One and Cooper filler cap ...

... can be changed to that of the Cooper S using a kit available from most MINI specialists.

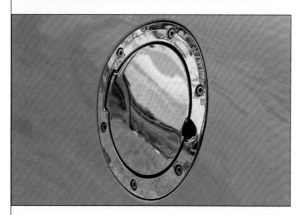

More radical changes to the filler cap look good, too. This one was produced by Mini Mania.

Right: A front spoiler adds a degree of meaness.

Far right: The spoiler from the side.

but a genuine black bumper mesh is available. Alternatively, suppliers such as Mini Speed can supply a sheet of mesh, which can be cut to size.

S type fuel cap conversion

Mini Spares and Mini Speed, amongst others, offer a Cooper S fuel cap conversion for non-S models, which uses genuine MINI parts and works with the car's central locking system. The kit will also fit the MINI One D, but on the diesel a replacement hinge is also needed – this is essential or the kit won't fit. The parts aren't available ready-painted and will require colour coding to match the finish of the car.

Front spoiler

For a different front-end look a DTM-style front spoiler can be fitted. These spoilers will fit all models of the original series new MINI and are precision moulded in ABS plastic. They're available in black, ready for painting if required to match the car's colour. A complete fitting kit is also supplied. An extrusion fits on the lower lip of the spoiler to protect the paintwork.

Rear roof spoiler

A rear roof spoiler is available for the MINI One, One D, Cooper and Cooper S. It's a very neat fitment, which is positioned just above the rear window and effectively forms a small extension to the rear of the roof. Needless to say, the spoiler won't fit onto the Convertible models. An alternative is available from John Cooper Works accessories, who produce a carbon fibre rear spoiler and also a tailgate handle to match. Hamann also make a rear roof spoiler, which fits on the tailgate but is a slightly different design from the BMW item.

Wheel arch extensions
Two designs of wheel arch extensions are available for those wishing to extend the arches further than the standard fitment plastic arch extensions. These are supplied by Mini Spares, who sell narrow arches with front and lower lips, or huge arches which go together with a body kit.

Other accessories
Roof bars
For those wishing to add to the luggage carrying capacity of the MINI, roof bars are available. No roof modifications or drilling are required.

Towbars
The MINI One, One D and Cooper models can be fitted with a very neat genuine MINI accessory towbar with an unbraked towing capacity of 500kg (1,100lb). With brakes on the trailer, the trailer-towing load can be increased to 650kg (1,435lb). This is very useful as the MINI has a very small boot capacity, and using a trailer is also a very good way of ensuring that the rear load area of the car isn't subject to too much wear and tear if dirty or bulky loads are often carried. Unfortunately, the towbar cannot be fitted to Cooper S models because of the positioning of the twin centre-exit exhaust pipes – unless of course the exhaust system is changed for a side-routed aftermarket performance item.

The sill covers …

… and bumpers are easily removed from the MINI.

This means that body kits, such as the genuine MINI Aero Kit, are easily fitted.

Far left: The side sills from the Aero Kit.

Left: The rear view of the Aero. This is a JCW Works special.

Sometimes wheels and an Aero Kit say it all.

Suspension height and wheels

Although suspension height and wheel style are fully covered in the chapter on suspension, they're worth mentioning again here as they do have a dramatic effect upon the overall appearance of the MINI. Lowered suspension is a vital part in creating a 'racier' look, and the wider wheels will create a broader more aggressive appearance. After all, the height of the bodyshell is determined by the diameter of the wheels and tyres, and the suspension height. Both of these factors must be taken

into consideration when deciding what modifications to carry out to the bodywork, and are particularly relevant to the following section on body kits.

Body kits

There's no doubt that the most dramatic changes to the appearance of a MINI will be brought about by the fitting of a body kit. Body kits are certainly not to everyone's taste, although the available kits range from fairly mild styling enhancements, such as the genuine

Right: Side grilles are easily changed …

Far right: … for a different look.

Variation on the mild body kit theme on the Mini Speed MINI.

MINI Aero kit, through to radical styled kits such as those produced by Zeemax. The genuine MINI Aerodynamics Package, or Aero Kit as it's generally known, was quite a popular fitment to new MINIs and is also popular as a retro-fit modification. Two types of Aero Kit are available, one for the One and Cooper models and one for the Cooper S. The Aero Kit does look good, and results in the MINI resembling a John Cooper Challenge race car, but to look at its best on all of the MINI models the Aero Kit must be fitted in conjunction with lowered suspension – the John Cooper lowering kit will lower the MINI by just the right amount for this kit. The Aero Kit is supplied in primer, ready to paint. It consists of front and rear bumpers, side skirts, mesh inserts for front and back, and all necessary fitting brackets. Some MINI specialists will supply the kit painted in the colour of your choice ready for fitting. It's worth noting that different versions of the Aero Kit are required for Minis fitted with Park Distance Control. Alternative exterior styling kits are made by Hamann; these

Rear view of the Mini Speed MINI.

Rear lower styling on a Mini Mania MINI.

Discreet John Cooper signature adds class.

Bolder Cooper decals are also available.

The *Carzone* is a full body kit with front and rear bumpers, side skirts, and front and rear arches. *CHD Tuning's* full body kit consists of front and rear bumpers (in this kit the front and rear bumpers don't come with mesh), front grille, side skirts and rear spoiler. This kit is reputed to fit well; it's made of high-quality fibreglass and comes ready for spraying. Panel fixings will need to be modified in order to fit the kit.

The *La Vacca* wide arch body kit for new MINI has wider arches than standard to allow larger wheels to be fitted. Nineteen-inch wheels can be used with this kit. The extra-width arches can be filled out by wheels with greater offset, or wheels fitted with spacers. Perhaps the best-known full body kits are those made by Zeemax. *Zeemax* produce their CSR and CSS conversions, both of which are body kits made to fit all new MINI models. The basic kit comprises front bumper, rear bumper, both side skirts, all four wheel arches, and a mesh kit. Zeemax body kits are superb quality and they fit properly too; they're manufactured in reinforced composite to the highest standard. The kits are not only visually stunning but are also aerodynamically functional. Zeemax conversions allows for the fitting of 17in, 18in or 19in wheels. All body kits require painting to match the colour of the car, and are generally a specialist job to fit. A poorly fitted body kit will not only look dreadful, it can also be dangerous.

include a front spoiler for the MINI One and Cooper, a spoiler for the Cooper S and a rear apron to suit the twin central exhaust of the S.

Other available non-genuine body kits include the following:

Woody.
(Castagna
Milano)

Coachbuilt MINIs

Coachbuilding and Minis have gone together since the mid-1960s. The new MINI has also received attention from the coachbuilders, most notably by Castagna Milano in Italy who produce conversions based on the MINI Cooper and Cooper S. Shortly after the MINI was introduced, they produced a 'Woody' countryman estate version reminiscent of the original 1960s Austin Mini Countryman. The quality of this company's conversions is stunning and it's reflected in the price. Very nice if you can afford it.

Right: Crossup.
*(Castagna
Milano)*

Far right:
Hybrid.
*(Castagna
Milano)*

Right: Mini
MINI. *(Castagna
Milano)*

Far right:
Shortened MINI.
*(Castagna
Milano)*

SUWagon.
*(Castagna
Milano)*

Far left top:
SUWagon front.
*(Castagna
Milano)*

Far l eft bottom:
SUWagon rear.
*(Castagna
Milano)*

Tender 2.
*(Castagna
Milano)*

Tender 1.
*(Castagna
Milano)*

Colour-coding of the wheel arches and sills gives a smoother appearance to the car.

Painting

A new MINI takes ten hours to paint in the factory in a seven-stage process that also applies protective coatings and water-based varnishes. The completed bodyshell is cleaned to remove any unwanted particles that are present following the assembly and welding. Once clean, the entire body is dipped and zinc phosphate coated, after which the first priming coat of paint is applied by means of cathodic electrodeposition, which is the basis for permanent protection against corrosion. The body is then coated with a surfacer primer, after which it's cleaned again by a mechanical duster. The colour top coat is applied, then the body is coated with a two-pack clear coat. As a result of all this, any repainting of large areas of damaged or modified MINI bodywork should be carried out by a high quality bodyshop which is able to replicate the factory finish.

In the past it wasn't uncommon to respray a car after about five years, often in a completely different colour. Today, complete colour change treatment is reserved for out-and-out custom vehicles, as on more conventionally or lightly modified cars a colour change usually means a reduction in the car's value.

Colour coding

A popular and look-enhancing mod is to colour code the side skirts, wheel arch extensions and front and rear bumper aprons. It's a straightforward and reasonably inexpensive way of giving the MINI smoother lines, and some specialists will supply pre-painted parts for fitting at home. The components need to be completely flatted down to remove all texture and then prepared to produce a smooth mirror finish for painting. The only downside of this mod is that the painted components will show

It looks particularly good with the right wheels.

Smooth lines of the painted MINI side skirt.

any minor car park dings and scratches a great deal more than the original black parts.

Bodywork maintenance

Regular cleaning of the bodywork is essential to maintain a MINI in top condition. Polishing every three to six months, depending upon how often and where the car is used, will also make a considerable difference. A range of polishes is available from BMW and there are some really excellent aftermarket polishes, a good example being Meguiars. Find one that is right for you and your MINI and use it regularly. A MINI isn't a large car and can be maintained in top condition with relatively little time spent on it. For a quick spruce up, a car wash shampoo that includes wax polish can work wonders, although the car will need to be rinsed fully and leathered off to prevent streaking as it dries. If the car is in daily use, a weekly wash is going to be required. If it's not possible to wash the whole car, at least try to wash the wheels. This is very important if expensive alloys are fitted, especially those with a polished finish. Leaving brake dust on alloys will cause them to rapidly deteriorate, resulting in the surface lacquer breaking down and

corrosion setting in; washing them weekly will go a long way to slow down the deterioration, and will also have the benefit of making the whole car look reasonably clean even when the rest of the body is slightly dirty.

Small scratches and scuffs on the paintwork can often be removed with a scratch-removing compound. It will usually be necessary to polish the whole panel afterwards to restore shine. Stone chips and larger scratches should be touched in quickly to prevent rusting. If you don't feel confident doing this, some BMW dealers have a minor bodywork clinic to repair scratches and to remove small dents without having to repaint the panel. Alloy wheel chips and scuffs, provided they aren't too bad, can also be repaired. There are, as well, a number of mobile companies who specialise in this type of repair.

Headlamp protection

MINI headlamps are very expensive to replace, and clear headlamp protectors make a great deal of sense. MINI accessories protectors are made of soft material to absorb the impact from stones and gravel – an inexpensive way to protect the headlamps, but they're only available for headlights without washers.

the interior

The MINI is as distinctive inside as it is outside. There's a bold retro interior theme which follows the lines of the original Mini with a centrally-mounted speedometer and central bank of switches. The level of trim is good, even in the basic versions; and higher spec models, particularly those with leather seat upgrades, can be quite luxurious. Being a two-door car, rear seat access is achieved by a front seat tilting mechanism that tilts and slides the seat forward in one movement. There's a memory function that returns both the backrest and cushion to the starting position when the squab is pushed back. This can take a little mastering as it's easy to apply insufficient pressure and return the backrest to the correct position leaving the seat staying forward. The bucket-type rear seats provide a very low seating position. Rear armrests are integrated in the side trim.

Cloth/leather combination upholstery was available as an option on all models. This included a leather steering wheel and gearknob, plus lumbar support on the One, One D and Cooper where they weren't already standard equipment. A large number of Cooper Ss are fitted with the optional leather upholstery, the choices of which include two Satellite cloth/leather combinations and two Gravity full leather upholstery designs.

The central air vents mimic the two additional instruments from the early Cooper and Super De Luxe Mini three-instrument oval binnacle. The MINI One D, Cooper and S models are fitted with a rev counter as standard, which is located in front of the driver on the steering column. If the optional navigation system was ordered, the speedo was relocated next to the rev counter, with the satellite navigation display taking its place in the central dial. The steering wheel is height-adjustable, and on the Cooper models there's a multifunction steering wheel option giving direct operation of the stereo system and cruise control when fitted.

All models in the MINI range are fitted with driver, front passenger and side airbags as standard. The front airbags interact with the seat belt latch tensioners and the belt force limiters, and inflate according to the severity of an accident. There's also an optional head airbag system – the Advanced Head Protection System (AHPS).

The rear seats are fitted with three-point seat belts and adjustable headrests, and Isofix child seat fittings were also available as an option for those with young children.

Leather steering wheel

A good leather steering wheel should be considered an essential extra on all MINIs not so equipped as standard. A two-spoke leather steering wheel, which also came with a leather gear knob, could be specified on all MINI models except the Cooper S. The Cooper S is fitted with a sports leather steering wheel and gearknob as standard. A leather steering wheel and gearknob was included in the optional Pepper packs, and also with the cloth/leather and full leather upholstery options. A multifunction (see above) leather steering wheel was also available.

Right: A leather steering wheel is essential on a MINI.

Far right: Bespoke leather on a MINI wheel.

Far left: Racing
MINI looks low
and mean.

Left: Challenge
Cooper S with
Aero Kit.

cars across both of the classes. This is so
that all the competitors can be
accommodated at the same time on one
grid. Separate championship points are
awarded for each class. Points are also
awarded for the JCC Novice Championship,
and at the end of the season there's an
overall champion for the highest number of
points scored from either championship. All
the cars are sealed and policed at all events
to prevent any unauthorised modifications
being made.

All the MINIs taking part are built to a
road legal specification, meaning that in
theory they could be driven to the
event (on road tyres), raced and driven
home again.

Racing preparation

For the John Cooper Challenge, MINIs are
prepared to the following specifications.
These are the specifications for the 2007
racing year.

The same S
showing side
skirts and rear
apron.

Far left: Not all
racing body
mods are
desirable.

Left: Getting
dressed for
racing at the old
JCW Works in
East Preston.

MINI Challenge Cooper Club Class spec

Engine:	4-cylinder, 1598cc, gas-flowed and skimmed cylinder head
Max power:	133bhp @ 6,000rpm
Max torque:	123Nm @ 4,800rpm
Power to weight:	118bhp per ton
Bore/stroke:	88.5/77mm
Compression ratio:	10.6:1
Valve gear:	4 per cylinder
Ignition and fuel:	Siemens EMS engine management, sequential injection
Air filter:	K&N open filter, oiled
Exhaust:	421 manifold, Lowcell cat, straight through rear silencer, stainless steel, 92dba
Gearbox:	5-speed manual, standard
Final drive:	3.94:1
Suspension	
Front:	Bilstein struts, coil springs, height-adjustable, bump and rebound-adjustable, front anti-roll bar, fixed camber
Rear:	Bilstein coil-over springs, height-adjustable, bump and rebound-adjustable, rear anti-roll bar
Steering:	Rack-and-pinion, electric power assistance
Brakes	
Front:	273mm vented discs, single-pot sliding caliper, Mintex 1166F4R pads
Rear:	259mm discs, single-pot sliding caliper, Mintex 1144 type pads
Wheels:	Pepperpot alloy, 5.5x15in
Tyres:	Dunlop DO2G 195/55/R15 semi cit slick
Wet tyre:	CR9000/404 185/580/R15
Rollcage:	Safety Devices bolt-in 6-plate FIA-approved with removable side-bars
Fire extinguisher:	4-litre plumbed-in system, manually operated from inside and out by pull cables. FIA-approved
Battery isolator:	Electrical cut-out system that can be operated from inside and outside of vehicle. MSA-approved
Race seat:	Corbeau Revolution or Recaro or pro-series Kevlar compound mix. FIA-approved
Seatbelt harness:	Luke seat belt harness, 5- or 6-point fixings, quick release FIA-approved.

MINI Challenge Cooper S Class spec

Engine:	4-cylinder, 1598cc, Eaton Type 5 supercharger, ported and skimmed cylinder head
Max power:	210bhp @ 6,950rpm
Max torque:	245Nm @ 4,500rpm
Power to weight:	175bhp per ton
Bore/stroke:	88.5/77mm
Compression ratio:	8.3:1
Valve gear:	4-per cylinder single overhead cam
Ignition and fuel:	Siemens EMS engine management, sequential injection
Air filter:	Full-flow Pipercross
Exhaust:	Stainless steel rear silencer, straight through
Gearbox:	6-speed Getrag manual, standard
Final drive:	2.74:1 or 2.81:1 Quaife LSD
Suspension	
Front:	Bilstein struts, coil springs, height-adjustable, bump and rebound-adjustable, front anti-roll bar, fully-adjustable camber
Rear:	Bilstein coil-over springs, height-adjustable, bump and rebound-adjustable, rear lower arm-adjustable, rear anti-roll bar
Steering:	Rack-and-pinion, electric power assistance
Brakes	
Front:	300mm vented discs, alloy 4-pot caliper, Mintex 1166F4R/F2R pads
Rear:	259mm discs, single-pot sliding caliper, Mintex 1144 type pads
Hoses:	Goodridge braided
Wheels:	Alloy Cross spoke, 6.5x16in
Tyres:	Dunlop DO2G 205/55/R16 slick
Wet tyre:	CR9000/404 210/605/R16
Roll cage:	Safety Devices bolt-in 6-plate FIA-approved with removable side-bars and padding
Fire extinguisher:	4-litre plumbed-in system, manually operated from inside and out by pull cables. FIA-approved
Battery isolator:	Electrical cut-out system that can be operated from inside and outside of vehicle. MSA-approved
Race seat:	Corbeau Revolution or Recaro or pro-series Kevlar compound mix. FIA-approved
Seatbelt harness:	Luke seat belt harness, 5- or 6-point fixings, quick-release FIA-approved.

rallying

There have been a number of privately-entered MINIs in rallying. Some have taken part in international events, but sadly there's been no works-backed team nor, as yet, any hint of one in the future. Companies that have prepared MINIs for rallying report that the car is very suitable once fully prepared. On the downside, it's quite a heavy car, but the weight does equal strength, making the MINI exceptionally durable in rough conditions. This is borne out by those MINIs that have competed in rallying emerging virtually unscathed at the end of the event.

In 2004, Northern Mini specialists Mini Sport announced their own New MINI Rally Championship to begin in 2005. Mini Sport have been rallying original Minis for over 30 years, and the Mini Sport Rally Championship was intended to be a low-budget series of ten rallies which would provide some very close competitive motorsport. The rally MINI Coopers were tuned to produce 140bhp, and the Cooper S tuned to 200bhp, and built to Group N specification. Mini Sport built and tested a car successfully, but no main sponsor could be found and the championship has so far not got off the ground.

Keeping the bonnet shut.

Rally preparation

Longer springs and more suspension travel are a must for serious rally work, and to prepare the car the shell must be stripped of all components. For the Mini Sport rally car the ground clearance was raised by 60mm over standard to gain that much-needed suspension travel and ground clearance, a 6mm-thick steel plate was welded in to the strut tops to both strengthen them and raise the platform. Longer, narrower springs were fitted. Bodyshell prep involved strengthening the shell by seam welding the bulkhead and front chassis legs, also seam welding the floor. A full Safety Devices roll cage was fitted; this in itself adding considerably to overall shell strength. All lines – fuel, brake,

Right: Rally MINI uses different type of bonnet fastener.

Far right: A similar method keeps the tailgate down.

Tow points on a competition MINI.

and battery – were run inside the car. Subframe strengthening was also deemed necessary. Bonnet pins prevented the bonnet from flying open and a carbon fibre four-lamp pod was added to the bonnet to house extra lighting.

Mechanical modifications included engine-tuning and gearbox modification. The ratios were changed to improve acceleration at the expense of some top speed, as the standard ratios are too high for stage rallying. The gear lever assembly was relocated inside the car to prevent damage from rocks under the car. The change mechanism was mounted on top of the 'transmission tunnel', and a shorter gear lever used. The brakes were upgraded by fitting alloy billet calipers to improve

braking and save weight, and an adjustable brake bias valve, to vary the pressure from front to rear, was also included. The handbrake was converted to hydraulic operation. Minilite wheels completed the rally spec.

Mini Sport supply a number of parts to convert MINIs to rally spec. These include Kevlar underfloor guards, which run the full length of the car, including under the fuel tank. A sump guard is an essential requirement for any type of off-road event, and several types are available. Competition rear mudflaps are also available.

Suitable tyres must be fitted for off-road events. The Mini Sport MINI was equipped with 185/65R15 Yokohama gravel tyres.

Far left: A full sump guard is essential for stage rallying.

Left: Some rally MINIs use steel wheels.

two of the best

All new MINIs lend themselves well to modification. Just how to go about modifying a MINI is very much down to the individual, but it will also be dictated by what the car is to be used for. Here are two examples of well tuned and well balanced MINI Cooper Ss. One has been built as a very fast road car which is also used by its owner for track days, while the other is an out-and-out race car.

one for the road

The fast road/race inspired look works very well with the MINI and more and more people are choosing to build fast-road MINIs along these lines. This particular MINI has been tuned very much along the lines of a JC Challenge Cooper S Class MINI, but with additional engine tuning. The car was built for its owner specifically for both fast-road use and track-day use. The suspension has been set to be slightly more road friendly than it would be on a race-only car, although the car sees slightly more track use than road use and if it was an everyday road car the ride height should be marginally higher. MINIs built along these lines can be tailored exactly to the owner's requirements, as there are no set limits on the level of tuning that can be carried out for track-day cars.

This car has a fast road/race inspired look and was built specifically for fast-road and occasional track-day use.

Specification

Engine
1598cc, Eaton Type 5 supercharger, ported & skimmed cylinder head, Pipercross air filter, stainless steel straight-through rear silencer. 225bhp @ 6950 rpm

Transmission
Six speed Getrag manual gearbox with 2.74:1 Quaife LSD

Brakes
Front:
300mm vented discs, alloy six-pot caliper, Mintex pads

Rear:
259mm discs, single-pot sliding caliper, Mintex pads, Goodridge braided hoses

Suspension
Front:
KW struts, coil springs, height-adjustable, bump and rebound adjustable, front anti-roll bar, fully adjustable camber.

Rear:
KW coil over springs, height-adjustable, bump and rebound adjustable, rear lower arm adjustable, rear anti-roll bar.

Wheels and Tyres
6.5x16 alloy Cross-spoke wheels.
Dunlop 205/55/R16 tyres

Interior
Corbeau Revolution seats,
Luke 5-point seat belt harness,
Safety Devices bolt-in roll cage

Exterior
MINI Aero bodykit, fully colour coded, rear spoiler

Extra bonnet fasteners are used to guard against the bonnet flying open at high speed.

This car features 6.5x16-inch alloy wheels with Dunlop 205/55R16 tyres.

The interior features a full roll cage, fire extinguisher switch and a race steering wheel…

… along with race seats and Luke 5-point harnesses.

The uprated intercooler works in conjunction with an Eaton Type 5 supercharger.

The modified engine, with ported and skimmed cylinder head, produces a healthy 225bhp.

one for the track

The livery leaves no doubt that this car is designed for track use.

The low stance and wide rubber adds to the purposeful look.

This is a well-prepared example of a MINI Challenge Cooper S Class spec race car. The overall specification is actually very similar to the road/track day MINI described previously, but the car has been built to comply with the exacting regulations of the JC Challenge. In line with regulations, the engine has been tuned to 210bhp Cooper Works spec, interestingly this is 15bhp less than the road MINI described previously. This particular car is not used on the road, but with a change to road-legal tyres and the relevant road tax/insurance and MoT, where applicable, all JC Challenge cars can be driven on the road.

The race steering wheel and data logging display indicate that this is a race car.

The race car also features a padded roll cage, a lap timer in the position normally occupied by the in-car entertainment unit and extra switch gear on the centre console.

The race car is also very much a single seater!

The modified engine produces 210bhp and features a ported and skimmed cylinder head and revised engine management system.

Specification

Engine
1598cc, Eaton Type 5 supercharger, ported & skimmed cylinder head, Siemens EMS engine management system, sequential injection. Full-flow Pipercross air filter, straight-through exhaust system with stainless-steel rear silencer.
210bhp @ 6950 rpm

Transmission
Gearbox: Six speed Getrag manual, standard
Final Drive: 2.74:1 Quaife LSD

Brakes
Front: 300mm vented discs, alloy four-pot caliper, Mintex 1166F4R/F2R pads. Rear: 259mm discs, single-pot sliding caliper, Mintex 1144 type pads. Hoses: Goodridge braided

Suspension
Front: Bilstein struts, coil springs, fully height, camber and caster adjustable, bump and rebound adjustable, front anti-roll bar.
Rear: Bilstein coil over dampers, height adjustable, bump and rebound adjustable, rear lower arm adjustable, rear anti-roll bar.

Wheels and Tyres
6.5x16 inch alloy Cross-spoke wheels,
Tyres: Dunlop DO2G 205/55/R16 Slick
Wet Tyre: CR9000/404 210/605/R16

Interior
Safety Devices bolt-in FIA-approved roll-cage with removable side bars and padding. FIA-approved four-litre plumbed-in fire extinguisher system, manually operated from inside and out by pull cables. FIA-approved battery isolator and electrical cut-out system can be operated from inside and outside of vehicle. FIA-approved Sparco race seat. FIA-approved Luke seat belt harness, six-point fixings, quick-release.

Exterior
MINI Aero body kit, rear spoiler, full racing decals

A plumbed-in fire extinguisher is fitted behind the driver's seat.

Full slick tyres provide vast amounts of grip on the track.

appendix

New MINI specialists

The following addresses, telephone numbers and internet details were believed correct at the time of going to press. However, as they are subject to change, no guarantee can be given for their continued accuracy.

This is not a complete list of MINI specialists, but includes those whose products and services have particular relevance to this book.

AmD Technik, Unit 6, Cliffside Trade Park, Motherwell Way, West Thurrock, Essex RM20 3LE. Telephone 01708 861827. Fax 01708 863031 Webiste: www.amdtechnik.com

Avonbar Racing, Avcon House, Bullocks Farm, Bullocks Lane, Takeley, Essex CM22 6TA Tel: 01279 873428 Fax: 01279 873427 Website: www.avonbar.com

Birds, Iver Lane, Uxbridge, Middlesex UB8 2JF Tel: 01895 810850 Website: www.birdsauto.com

Castagna Milano Website: www.castagnamilano.com

Cobra Superform Limited, Units D1 and D2, Halesfield 23, Telford, Shropshire TF7 4NY Tel: 01952 684020 Website: www.cobraseats.com

John Cooper Works, Website: www.johncooper.co.uk

Cooper Turbo Research & Development Inc, 139 N Pacific Street (Suite A-1), San Marcos, CA 92069, USA Tel: 760 591 0311

Induction Technology Group Ltd, Unit 5, Fairfield Court, Seven Stars Industrial Estate, Whitley, Coventry, West Midlands CV3 4LJ Tel: 02476 305386

Kent Performance Camshafts, Units 1–4 Military Road, Shorncliffe Industrial Estate, Folkestone, Kent CT20 3SP. Tel: 01303 248666. Email: kentcams@btinternet.com

K&N Filters (Europe) Ltd, John Street, Warrington, Cheshire WA2 7UB Tel: 01925 636950

MED, Unit 6, 238 Tithe Street, Leicester LE5 4BN. Tel: 0116 246 1641

Mini Mania Ltd, The Acorn Center, Unit 3, Station Road, Ampthill, Beds, MK45 2QP Telephone 01525 841733. Fax: 01525 841769 Website: www.minimaniauk.com

MINI Motorsport Centre, Unit 12 Western Road Garage, Western Road, Shoreham by Sea, Sussex Telephone 12373 446666 tony@minimotorsportcentre.com

Mini Spares Centre, Units 12 & 13, Cranbourne Industrial Estate, Cranboure Road, Potters Bar, Herts EN6 3JN Tel: 01707 607700 Fax: 01707 656786 Email: sales@minispares.com

Mini Speed, Units 4–5, Abbot Close, Oyster Lane, Byfleet, Surrey KT14 7JN Tel: 01932 400567 Fax: 01932 400565 Email: sales@minispeed.co.uk

Mini Sport Ltd, Thompson Street, Padiham Lancs BB12 7AP Tel: 01282 778731

Moss London, Hampton Farm Industrial Estate, Hanworth, Middlesex TW13 6DB Tel: 020 8867 2020 (Branches throughout UK) Website: www.moss-europe.co.uk

Newton Commercial, Eastlands Industrial Estate, Leiston, Suffolk IP16 4LL. Tel: 01728 832880 Fax: 01728 832881 Email: newtoncomm@anglianet.co.uk Website: www.newtoncomm.co.uk

Optima Batteries, 4 Leaf Batteries Ltd, Shrublands, Norwich Road, Carbrooke, Thetford, Norfolk IP25 6TJ Tel: 01953 883344

Piper Cams, 2 St John's Court, Ashford Business Park, Sevington, Ashford, Kent TN24 0SJ Tel: 01233 500200 Fax: 01233 500300

Pipercross Performance Air Filters, Units 4–6 Tenter Road, Moulton Park Industrial Estate, Northampton NN3 6PZ Tel: 01604 494945

P&L Minis, 34 High Street, Thurnscoe, Rotherham Tel: 01709 889922 Website: www.plmini.com

R T Quaife Engineering Ltd, Vestry Road, Otford, Sevenoaks, Kent TN14 5EL Tel: 01732 741144 Fax: 01732 741555 Website: www.quaife.co.uk

Safety Devices International Ltd, 1st Floor, Kininvie House, Fordham Road, Newmarket, Suffolk CB8 7AQ Tel: 01638 561047

Slark Race Engineering, Unit 2a, Bunas Park, Hollom Down Road, Lopcombe, Salisbury, Wilts SB5 12BP Tel: 01264 781403

Southern Carburetters and Injection, Unit 6, Nelson Trading Estate, Morden Road, Wimbledon, London SW19 3BL T el: 0208 540 2723 Fax: 0208 540 0857

Tech Del Ltd (Minilite Wheels), Unit 4A, Roughmoor Industrial Estate, Williton, Taunton, Somerset TA4 4RF Tel: 01984 631033

Webasto Hollandia UK Ltd, Unit 8D, Stockton Close, Minworth Industrial Estate, Sutton Coldfield, Birmingham B76 1DH Tel: 0121 313 1222 Website: www.webasto.co.uk

West Tuning, Unit 20, Thruxton Race Circuit, Hants SP11 8PW Tel: 01264 773839 Website: www.west-tuning.com

Wizards of Nos, TMC Group Ltd, Rands Lane, Armthorpe, Doncaster, South Yorkshire DN3 3ER Tel: 01302 834343 Website: www.noswizard.com

Wood and Picket Ltd, Unit 14, Faygate Business Centre, Faygate, Horsham, West Sussex RH12 4DN Tel: 01293 852100 Fax: 01293 852110 Website: www.woodandpicket.com

other books from Haynes Publishing

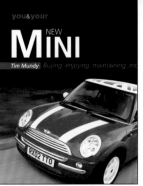

You & Your New MINI
Buying, enjoying, maintaining and modifying
by Tim Mundy
ISBN 978 1 84425 028 8
£17.99

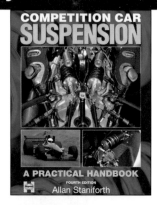

Competition Car Suspension
A practical handbook
by Allan Staniforth
ISBN 978 1 84425 328 9
£25.00

New MINI
(2nd Edition)
by Graham Robson
ISBN 978 1 84425 135 3
£17.99

Four-Stroke Performance Tuning
(3rd Edition)
by A. Graham Bell
ISBN 978 1 84425 314 2
£19.99

Engine Management Performance Tuning
Optimising carburettors, fuel injection and ignition systems
by Dave Walker
ISBN 978 1 85960 835 7
£17.99

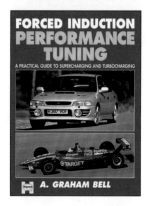

Force Induction Performance Tuning
A practical guide to supercharging and turbocharging
by A. Graham Bell
ISBN 978 1 85960 691 9
£25.00

Race and Rally Car Source Book
(4th Edition)
The guide to building or modifying a competition car
by Allan Staniforth
ISBN 978 1 85960 846 3
£19.99

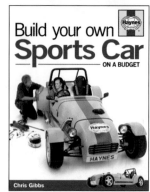

Build your own Sports Car on a budget
by Chris Gibbs
ISBN 978 1 84425 391 3
£17.99